Praise for *Fearless Referrals*

"Before I read Matt's book and started his referral coaching, I was asking by saying, 'I build my business by referral. Do you know of anyone I could help?' I would often get a 'let me think about that.' I also would get referrals that never materialized into meetings. With Matt's help, I have a method to get consistent referrals and am helping more new clients than ever before. In the past five months, I've generated over 40 new referrals, brought in 10 new clients, and have in excess of 100 million dollars in my newly built pipeline. Matt is the last guy I would refer to my competitors."

—*Stephen Lewis, Principal,*
Bernstein Global Wealth Management, Houston, TX

"The top Financial Planners would suggest that they get most of their business from client referrals. Research also suggests that most Financial Planners are not as effective as they might be in seeking client advocacy and turning a great service into more business opportunities. This book gets to the heart of what is required to add to your productivity and bottom line doing what you do best!"

—*Nick Cann, ACIB, CFP, Chief Executive,*
Institute of Financial Planning, Bristol, England

"I have lost count of the number of times in my 25-year career that I have been told, 'Don't forget to ask for referrals!' However, Matt is the *only person* who has ever taught me the who, what, when, where, and why of how to do so successfully."

—*Robert T. Watral, Financial Advisor,*
Ameriprise Financial Services, Inc., Raleigh, NC

"For those professionals who have struggled with—or aspire to improve—their business development results, here's a book that should be read, reread, and put into practice. *Fearless Referrals* contains step-by-step guidance to ask for, and obtain, more and higher quality referrals. Since implementing the Six Steps, my referral volume has at least doubled, with a significant increase in referral quality."

—*Eric Roddiger, Managing Director,*
Crutchfield Capital Corporation, Houston, TX

"I have been a practicing CPA and attorney for the past 43 years, but during the short period I have known Matt and read *Fearless Referrals*, my success rate has been dramatic, and, maybe more important, I have a lot more confidence in my ability to succeed. I have focused on a particular group of potential referrals—namely, CPA firm partners—and they have responded with quality referrals."

—*Michael H. Moss, Attorney at Law, Chicago, IL*

"Matt Anderson's *Fearless Referrals* is a true step-by-step guide to a process many salespeople find challenging. It covers not just asking for referrals, but the deeper concepts of earning referrals and a system to keep them coming. These are steps often left out by even seasoned professionals."

—Mike Ward, Regional Sales Manager,
US Bank—Business Banking, Milwaukee, WI

"*Fearless Referrals* helped my agents and me focus on existing, satisfied clients who were waiting to be asked to help. The practices in this book are transferable to any small business owner, and if the referral scripts and processes are implemented, they will undoubtedly affect gross income in a positive way . . . just as they have for many of the agents who I've worked with over the years."

—Tim Topoll, ChFC, CLU, CASL, Agency Field Executive,
State Farm Insurance, Madison, WI

"*Fearless Referrals* is the best business book I have read. It covers many aspects of how to run a successful business as well as simple techniques for getting referrals from clients. The most important lesson I learnt from Matt's book is to target the referrals you want. 'Feel free to recommend your friends and family' is too general. I listen to my clients and pick up on anyone that they talk about. Later, I will ask the client to recommend me to these specific people. This approach has worked for me with great success."

—Steven Barrett, Financial Planner,
Signature Financial Planning, Dublin, Ireland

"I received eight referrals the first time that I used the wisdom contained in *Fearless Referrals*. The book gives you an integrated step-by-step system to keep you on the path to get you the referrals that are there for the asking from your best clients. Reading this book and creating your written referral script will increase your business over and above any other marketing activity that you are taking."

—Simon Reilly, Financial Advisor and Investment Advisor Coach,
Speaker & Writer, Leading Advisor, Inc.,
Parksville, British Columbia

"*Fearless Referrals* teaches you how to think and operate like a top referral-getter. The book makes an immediate difference in your mindset and your capability to positively enhance your client relationships while adding new prospects to your business. Read this book and be ready to take your life and business to the next level."

—John F Nichols, CLU, MSM, President, Disability Resource Group, Inc.

FEARLESS REFERRALS

Boost Your **Confidence**

Break Down Doors

Build a **Powerful Client List**

MATT ANDERSON

New York   Chicago   San Francisco   Lisbon   London
Madrid   Mexico City   New Delhi   San Juan
Seoul   Singapore   Sydney   Toronto

1 2 3 4 5 6 7 8 9 10   DOC/DOC   1 6 5 4 3 2 1

ISBN   978-0-07-178287-6
MHID   0-07-178287-7

e-ISBN   978-0-07-178288-3
e-MHID   0-07-178288-5

McGraw-Hill books are available at special quantity discounts to use as premiums and sales promotions, or for use in corporate training programs. To contact a representative please e-mail us at bulksales@mcgraw-hill.com.

This book is printed on acid-free paper.

To Mum

Contents

ACKNOWLEDGMENTS

For about three years I wanted to write a book but didn't believe I belonged on the same shelves as the authors I admired. Then I did start writing this book (well over three years ago) but got frustrated trying to make the time for it when I needed to be earning money and paying bills. I was not convinced it would make a difference for anyone.

I would not have completed this book for I don't know how long, had it not been because of a project I committed to in Landmark Education's Self-Expression and Leadership course in 2009. Thank you, Wayne Fetman, for your belief in me. The support of the people in this class and my making the verbal commitment to them made all the difference in giving me the incentive to follow through. I now understand why so many people have shared with me over the years, "Oh yeah, I want to write a book too. I just need to find the time!" It is not easy! And I didn't have a family to support, so I can empathize with any aspiring writer.

But this book did need writing, as referrals are what every business owner, salesperson, and professional responsible for generating business likes best. They are the ultimate compliment that says you have done a good job and another person is endorsing you.

I have now spent more than nine years helping people bring in more referral business, and the results I get with my coaching clients create the urgency for me to get this information out to you so you can reap the rewards as well.

I am grateful to many inspiring business and personal development minds without whom I would never have survived in business to put me back on track on the rough days. Stephen Covey and Brian Tracy are the two most prominent, but the reinforcement I got from everyone listed in my bibliography only proves to me that we all need frequent support from many sources. Thank you to you all: your writing made a difference.

My own networking experiences and endless cups of coffee (and beers) have taken me all over not only the United States but the United Kingdom and even parts of Canada and the Middle East. I have learned from at least seven chamber of commerce memberships, leadership training in England and the United States with Business Network International, NAIFA's LILI program, multiple other leads groups, dozens of other networking events, hundreds of seminars and workshops with a wide variety of professions, the boards and committees on which I have served, and even my share of network marketing events.

But my best referral learning has come from doing it myself first and then coaching others how to get the same results. I have learned from so many, ranging from the great successes to those who could not get off square one—and everyone in between. Never a dull moment! Thank you to all those who have trusted me with their hard-earned income.

While I cannot mention everyone who deserves the thanks for helping me along the way, a final special thank-you:

- To Mum for your support long before anyone else thought I would make it. Thank you for your patience. I have finally learned how powerful it is to be supported. You have been telling me since I was little that I would go places and make an impact on the world. You have no idea how important those words of encouragement have meant.

- To the happy memory of my father, Pop. I know you're still around waiting to pick me up from somewhere or other. Your modeling of dependability and respectful treatment of others has helped me so much in life.

- ◆ To my wife, Erica, who has been the greatest support to me ever since we met. You are my inspiration.

- ◆ To my original editor, Angie Finch, for putting so much effort into this book and doing outstanding work on it. It was a pleasure working with you and so easy. Sorry we couldn't meet when I spoke in Atlantic City a while ago. I hope anyone interested in working with "the best" will contact you at ahfinch@optonline .net—I could not recommend anyone more highly!

- ◆ To Hugh Mason for giving me your undying friendship, for being my best man, and for opening the first doors for me in the United Kingdom and at McGraw-Hill. Who would have thought that the Fifth Concerto and *The Young Adult* would take us here!

- ◆ To Mark Mantell and John Gray at New York Life for believing in my work earlier than any other company on a national level. It was terrific fun coming to New York to record the training videos. I will never forget those opportunities, although I can't understand why you didn't like the Cheesehead! None of this would have happened without Eric Heiting, who made the first introduction. Thanks, Eric!

- ◆ To Scott Downs at MetLife for believing in my work and committing to results over the long haul. It has been a great experience, and I truly appreciate the faith you have in me.

- ◆ To Juli McNeely, Mike Smith, Susan Linck, Liz Pollock, and everyone at NAIFA–Wisconsin for accepting me—an outsider—and allowing me to get involved and be part of a great association.

- ◆ To Sean Bailey at Horsesmouth.com for taking me on as a contributing author in 2007 and publishing my writing ever since. This boosted my confidence that I belonged on a national stage.

- ♦ To Nick Cann at the IFP and Neil Denton at Standard Life for being open to helping me get established in the United Kingdom based on a bio I wrote extolling my own virtues!

- ♦ To Steve Lewis and Michael Ellington at Bernstein for starting such a rewarding business relationship. Steve, thanks for recommending me to the entire population of Texas!

- ♦ To Simon Reilly for providing your personal coaching and for opening doors to me in Canada so I can contribute there.

- ♦ To Steve Garrison for inspiring me to get the book completed. Your sharing about how you were doing the same pushed me on the days I thought I should do something else with my time. Good luck with your book, *The Five Secrets from Oz*!

Introduction

I am writing this book because I want you to know that you can grow a business successfully through referrals—and you already know how rewarding that can be; otherwise you would not have picked this book up. It is not easy, and I want you to know *that* right up front, too. I am not going to fill your head with false hype that you will have referrals coming out of your ears after Chapter 1. I know we all want something that's easy, but getting to that point will take most of you some time to accomplish. Eventually, you can get easy referrals—once you have the skill set.

And this is what really excites me so much: there *is* a way to grow your business by word of mouth. It is readily available to you. And you don't need to be great looking or have the gift of gab to do it. You do not have to be a natural at building spectacular relationships or have the personality of a Santa Claus. You don't even need a dynamic sense of humor or white teeth or a full head of hair.

What is in this book *works*. It will work for you if you follow what I suggest. And if it doesn't work, it is partly because of the challenge.

Here is the challenge: Many people who start their own business or go into sales do so because they like the independence. That's great—however, you don't need to reinvent every wheel because you see yourself as a do-it-yourselfer. I speak from the painful experience of someone who tried for many years! Simply follow what is recommended in this book and believe you have the ability too, and you will get faster results. I promise.

I also want you to know that on my journey to learning what I share in this book, I have made all the same mistakes everyone else has. I am a fairly introverted and shy Englishman living in the United

States. I used to be a conservative no-risk-taking elementary and middle school teacher who liked his steady paycheck and benefits.

But I was also one of those people who was always thinking of business ideas and then letting the voice in my head instantly talk me out of it, reminding me that I should stick to my safe place and put up with being surrounded by a majority of peers (not all) who could not wait for Friday to come along. Yet I felt a bit of a failure in front of the children sometimes—coming to the realization that my life experience was from studying but not really from doing much. I had this increasing sense that I was not living life or fulfilling my potential.

Well I finally got so unhappy as a teacher, working too many hours and feeling burned out on people, that I left the profession and stumbled around for two years not quite sure what to do next. Then a former girlfriend from Russia got in touch, and, not having any better ideas, I thought I might get a teaching certificate so I could go there and work. This was a foolproof idea until about a week later when I realized I was tired of teaching, I had not enjoyed being in Moscow when I had visited, and I really was not in love with this woman!

I will never forget how miserable I was that March lunchtime lying on my stomach on the same bed that my father had spent his last months on when he was dying from cancer at 58. I was completely stuck and thoroughly down in the dumps.

The one habit that saved me was buying personal development books. That afternoon my mother and I went to Leamington Spa, and on the upstairs floor of Waterstone's I picked a book off a shelf called *Be Your Own Life Coach* by Fiona Harrold. I had no idea what a life coach was, but her book felt like an IV of both adrenaline and inspiration for me. She talked about building confidence and starting your own business and taking responsibility for your life. She had me clean up my past and start believing in myself and believing that what I wanted was possible.

Perhaps for the first time since the encouragements my mother uttered to me during childhood, I began to say to myself, "Maybe I can do it." It was exactly what I needed, and it gave me the burst of self-confidence to get back on a plane to the United States, move to a completely new area (the mountains of New Mexico), and start my first business enterprise (which failed by the way, but that's for another story!).

I started on square minus one, quite frankly. Other than a grandfather who ran many different business enterprises before I knew him, including a fish and chip shop, but who ended up working in a department store in his sixties (that seemed to be more the butt of jokes), there were no business role models in my family. Everybody was an educator or factory worker of some kind.

I moved next to the mountains of New Mexico in 2002, which was exciting and quite foolish. Little did I know that New Mexico was the third poorest state in the Union at the time. Little did I know that when you are starting a business, it helps to know people! I knew nobody in a city of 750,000. So I networked like a madman. I joined two business leads groups, a gym, a chamber of commerce, and a Toastmasters chapter. I read as many books as I could get my hands on and started a second business (which also failed)!

And everywhere I went, I asked people where they got their business. What struck me was how almost everyone I asked would say "word of mouth." I was hoping people would mention specific places I could go to get business, but it was always this idea that other people spoke highly of them and opened doors to new business. No people ever said, "Oh, it was this ingenious direct mail campaign I did" or "Radio advertising"—I suppose they wouldn't have been networking if that were true.

I was intrigued. But what I quickly found out was that most professionals from all walks of life were talking about unsolicited referrals—ones they had not asked for—when they talked about "word of mouth," *and* that this was not enough to live on! In addition, not only were most people not asking for referrals, but they didn't know what to say to get them! A lot of people were not really doing anything to earn referrals either. They were just doing the same job everyone else in their industry was doing (they had just never stopped to notice or admit such a possibility).

I started talking to managers and trainers to find out what kind of help their salespeople were getting. This was interesting, too. A few had some kind of training system they had tried, but it seldom stuck. Sometimes some managers had found a way to get referrals, but their way didn't seem to work for their teams. Mostly there was no training. Or the person at the top would say something unhelpful, like "Well, all they need to do is ask!" as if the solution were always that simple. Maybe it worked in the 1970s.

I had stumbled onto something that was really important to salespeople and yet was hardly being addressed! For myself, I was very scared to cold-call, but I so liked the idea of running my own business that my mind raced (mostly out of desperation) to find ways to get more referrals just so I could stay in business. Because I networked so much, I started to train groups in how to network and get referrals—it didn't take that long to have something useful to share. That's the first time I learned about "the challenge."

I would present to a group a few ideas on what they could do to get more referrals, and then six weeks later I would return to cover a different topic. But invariably what I would find when I returned was that one or two people had made some changes in educating others how to refer them and that the remainder of the room consisted of a group of stubborn do-it-yourselfers who had ignored my suggestions so they could prove to themselves that they could figure it out for themselves—and they usually failed.

Still it's not all from being too independent. Some of the skill in getting referrals is counterintuitive, and some of it can feel a little labor intensive. So do you want results or the same old same old?

You know by now that getting referrals is not a quick fix or a software program. *If it were easy, everyone would get lots of referrals.*

In a recent book titled *Talent Is Overrated*, author Geoff Colvin argues that high performers in every field pursue *deliberate practice* in areas that address specific skills that take them *around* their limitations.

As Colvin effectively summed up:

> *If the activities that led to greatness were easy and fun, then everyone would do them, and they would not distinguish the best from the rest. The reality that deliberate practice is hard can even be seen as good news. It means that most people won't do it. So your willingness to do it will distinguish you all the more.*

This is what you need to do if you want more referral business—deliberate practice. And I'd like to commend you for taking the first step: proactively improving your referral skills by reading this book.

What Are Your Results for Getting Referrals?

I recently conducted a seminar and asked the audience to share what they already knew about getting referrals. Their list was long, including ideas such as ask for referrals, provide good customer service, build trust, add value, build relationships, follow up promptly, know your stuff, develop friendships, and use an agenda.

Next I asked the group for a show of hands of those who knew the rules of football. Many hands went into the air, so I asked whether we should all get together and scrimmage the nearest NFL team.

I got some rather strange looks. The point is, just because you know *how* to do something doesn't mean you have the commitment to follow through, the stamina to do what is necessary, and the stick-to-itiveness that is required.

You're getting my point, right? Many of the people at this seminar were not there because they did not know many of the important factors that help us all get referrals. It's quite possible they *thought* they didn't know. But they did. So what are the determining factors? It's likely that you too already know many of the important ways to get referrals, but are your results disappointing? What do you need to do differently? That's what this book is for.

Here are a few tips to get the most out of this book:

- **Schedule time to review what you've learned and practice it right away!** If you are scheduling time to read professionally, you are already in a tiny percentage of the business world. Congratulations. Very few people continue to grow by going the extra inch on a daily basis. However, it's not what you know; it's what you do with what you know that counts.

- **Take notes either on the inside cover pages of this book or somewhere you can revisit easily.** *Please*, write all over the pages; highlight helpful passages. Make this a tool, not a museum piece.

- **Schedule the final few minutes of your reading time to consider ideas you want to implement.** If you have 30 minutes set aside for reading, use the last 5 minutes to review your notes or highlighted areas and decide how you're going to use these ideas.

- **Revisit all your notes on a regular basis and look for ways to take action.** Rather than launching into yet another book, go back through your notes on a monthly basis.

- **Practice what sounds useful as soon as possible.** Action is the only way to improve your skills—and your results.

As you read this book, keep asking yourself, "How can I implement this into my own business?" Don't wait to start using what you learn here to get more referrals. It's never too early to put your radar out for happy clients who may be ready to refer you to others.

The sooner you start using these ideas, the sooner you can hone them to fit your personality.

You may need to hear an idea 10 to 30 times (sometimes more) before the light goes on. I think this point is not emphasized enough. Do you ever take action on a brand-new idea the first time you hear it? It's very rare. Hearing an idea once seldom raises enough credibility in our minds for us to take action. Most of us need to hear something multiple times before we will ever do anything and the lightbulb goes on.

Why do most high achievers recommend that you read their book multiple times? I'm embarrassed to admit I used to think it was because their egos were too big. "I'll decide if your ideas are any good; I don't need to do that," I said to myself. "I don't have time for that!" And then I'd hurry on to read something else and miss a lot of important ideas.

Certainly, we should question everything we hear, and it does need to fit who we are; but virtually the oldest adage out there is *if you want to be successful, do what successful people do.* I recommend that you engrain this material by revisiting it regularly: you will get more referrals!

Fearless Referrals is structured to help you define your own value and develop conversations that are comfortable and effective for you to leverage increasingly more relationships into more and better business opportunities. The book is divided into seven chapters.

Chapter 1 covers the Fearless Referral fundamentals—what does it take to get referrals, given that it is not as easy as some would have us think?

Chapter 2, "Earning the Fearless Referral," acknowledges our role in putting enough water in the well in relationships such that others are willing to open doors for us.

Chapter 3 is called "Becoming Fearless," and it addresses how we get in our own way and offers different solutions to getting past that.

Chapter 4, entitled "Fearless Referral Asking," crushes the place where most people play too small and are too bashful and shows you how to exercise your asking muscle so that you can have the business you want.

Now that the horse is in front of the cart, now that you are mentally ready to expect people to help you, Chapter 5 has seven nuts-and-bolts sections on fearless referral-getting strategies.

Chapter 6—"The Six Steps to a Fearless Referral Conversation"— highlights what to say. These six steps will help you find wording that works and is nonthreatening and conversational.

The final chapter, "Fearless Referral Follow-Up," closes the loop between all the productive work you've done so far and vital follow-up steps—tracking your results and opportunities, asking for more, setting bigger goals, and honoring referral sources—so that you instill your progress into lifelong business habits.

CHAPTER I

The Fearless Referral Fundamentals

We are about to enter the age of word-of-mouth ... even in this age of mass communication and multi-million dollar advertising campaigns, [it] is still the most important form of human communication.

—Malcolm Gladwell, *The Tipping Point*

5–15–50–80

H ow exactly do I define a *referral*?

Referral. A referral is when your referral source (Person A) recommends you to Person B because Person A is really pleased with the work you have done.

In other words, you are being recommended for all the right reasons because you have done a good job. There is nothing cheesy or borderline manipulative going on.

Not All Referrals Are Created Equal

One fact we have to acknowledge right away is that the quality of referrals can vary a lot! How enthusiastically people communicate about you and how strong the relationships are between you and Person A, and between Person A and Person B, make a huge difference.

The lowest-quality referral is when you are given the name and number of Person B and he or she is not expecting your call. Because these referrals are so poor in quality in this day and age, this book is not going to spend time on clever techniques to generate a list of names. That is not an effective word-of-mouth endorsement.

Person B should want to talk to you—or at least be open to hearing from you!

You want to get your referral prospects warmed up so that they actually want to hear from you! That's how to run a business that works, is fun, and is based on developing quality relationships.

Why is it so important to have a prospect expecting your call? What's wrong with just calling someone and name-dropping with this unsuspecting person (apart from the fact that you don't like it when it's done to you!)?

The Sandler Sales Institute studied this several years ago, and my experience over the years has found the institute's numbers to be remarkably accurate. Here's how often the following turned into *business* (not just an appointment):

- **5 percent.** At best the amount of business you'll get from cold calls.

- **15 percent.** The amount of business you'll get when you use someone's name and say, "Sarah Megson gave me your name"—but your call is *not* expected. And that person may be a little puzzled why Sarah had never mentioned anything. To the person receiving the call, it feels like a cold call. Many people get suspicious.

- **50 percent.** The amount of business you'll get *when you have permission to call*; *your call is expected*; you say, "Sarah Megson suggested I call"; and the recipient replies, "Oh, yes, that's right. Yes, she did tell me."
- **80 percent.** The amount of business you'll get *when you are personally introduced.*

Clearly, there are variations on the quality of a personal introduction. Being introduced briefly by chance in the hallway of an office is obviously not as powerful as the three of you scheduling to meet for lunch.

TIPS

Two great tips for responding to a lead who was expecting your call:

Your first question should be, "How did it come up in the conversation?"

Your next question is, "Good. Actually I'm curious. What did Sarah share with you?" What the person tells you is tremendously informative, as often people do not know as much as you think. They are talking to you out of respect for the referral source. And it gives you time to think about which direction to take the call.

LESSONS TO LEARN

You don't just want a long list of names, none of whom are expecting your call. Unless you're a cold-calling maestro, you're virtually wasting your time.

Certainly some names that you mention to a referral will carry more weight than others. If these two people have known each other for 25 years, that will help a lot. If the CEO is recommending you to one of her vice presidents, that will make a difference (although still a loaded one). But *rarely* does just having a name work as much as we'd like to think. I am uncomfortable being given just a name and a number because it so seldom leads to business. It never ceases to amaze me how most people think just mentioning their name will make all the difference and how they are usually mistaken!

What you always want to aim for is to ask your referral source (Person A) to warm up his or her referral (Person B) by talking to Person B briefly or finding out via e-mail whether Person B would be interested in a quick conversation.

You want someone else to go to bat for you.

Another advantage of this is that you will avoid one of those meetings where someone has agreed to meet you who has *no idea* what you do and why he or she is meeting you.

The best kind of referral to get is, without question, the personal introduction—lunch, coffee, or a beer after hours works best. When someone personally introduces you to a prospect, 80 percent of the time the business will happen. Why? Because it gives people a chance to get comfortable with you. Their actions speak volumes for your credibility. Clearly, we save these requests for bigger fish. Revisit your prospect list and decide whom you would like to meet in person.

BELIEVE 100 PERCENT IN THE BENEFITS OF ASKING FOR REFERRALS

The stronger you believe in building a referral business, the more committed you will be to getting outstanding results and to asking for referrals.

Why are referrals so great? Why are they such a wonderful way to build, sustain, and grow your business?

Here's a list of reasons:

1. **Asking for and getting more referrals will help you become more assertive.** Assertiveness is a *wonderful* quality. As you start getting results in one area, it will encourage you then to ask for other things: you will ask for more business from the same person (more of the person's assets?), you will ask prospects to get off the fence, and you will expect centers of influence to reciprocate. *Assertive is good!*

2. **Asking for and getting more referrals will help you be more opportunistic.** This is a priceless skill to keep honing. We can always get sharper and become more aware of all the ways we can help those in our network. Strive to continue improving in this area.

3. **Sometimes you just have to show up sober.** A quality referral is the absolute strongest marketing tool you can find. People listen to someone when they trust that person's opinion. When someone has given you a really good referral, many of your prospects come presold, and all you need to explain is how and when the work can get started. I love these meetings!

4. **Referrals give you more independence and more control over your business.** Why? Because you need people who know, like, and trust you to get referrals. This requires building and maintaining strong relationships. Once you are making a habit of this and you are keeping in touch with your client base, you can always tap in to your resource-rich business because you have been making the "emotional bank account deposits" (see Chapter 2). This provides the foundation for a stable business, which is a much more enjoyable business lifestyle for you.

5

5. **Working with referrals is about helping others—a client-centered approach—when done right.** The right approach is when your "referral conversation" is focused on your referral sources' helping people they care about—not some "me, me, me" act of desperation. If your referral sources can see that you are sincerely concerned about the welfare of people they care about, they will take the spirit of your request seriously. Difficult though this is when you need business yesterday, you must focus on helping others first. Take that leap of faith and your rewards will come.

   The good news is that recent research supports the client-centered approach. In Andy Sernovitz's *Word of Mouth Marketing,* he found that *the two main reasons why others recommend you are because they like to help people they care about and because it makes them feel good!* Neither of these reasons has anything to do with you. Your clients are not motivated to see you drive a nicer car, take more time off, or have plastic surgery!

6. **Referrals are great for people who dislike selling and aren't very skilled at it.** Now someone else is "selling" you beforehand. It allows you to focus on building quality relationships. The business and referrals will come, provided you ask for what you want (see Chapter 4).

7. **Referrals increase your integrity and enhance your reputation.** Why? New business comes from real people, not clever advertising or marketing gimmicks. Additionally, you won't have to depend on these things to get new business. If you aren't doing a good job, nobody will recommend you. The fact that you get your business from referrals speaks volumes about the quality of your work and what others think of you. Others are putting their integrity on the line to endorse you. That's the kind of business people trust and the kind of endorsement others listen to. It's a wonderful way to be—personally and professionally.

8. **You get to clone your best clients.** Often you get referred to people who have similar personalities to that of your referral source. Most people will not refer you unless they like you. This is especially wonderful if you like your clients, because the chances are that they'll refer you to people similar to themselves.

   Not long ago I was introduced to the friend of a client. Originally he had told me that if his buddy didn't call me back right away, I was to "tell him Brian will come over and kick his a**!" (I didn't use that line, although I was tempted.) I had a hard time keeping a straight face when we met. This friend was remarkably similar in personality to the client: friendly, energetic, talkative, enthusiastic, and he had a good sense of humor. The meeting went great. (See reason 1.) Sometimes this feels like the biggest win there is to your referral business.

9. **It's easier to recommend someone else than to "sell yourself."** People listen to third-party endorsements more than you trying to persuade them that you're the best there is. Almost all people have others in their lives whose opinions they respect and whom they look up to and often follow.

10. **It's easier to leverage a good relationship to get business than to advertise, cold-call, or buy leads.** Consumers are getting increasingly cynical. They expect you to have an agenda that does not sincerely put them first—unless a trusted person is recommending you.

11. **You can make more money by saving on other marketing expenses.** When you can master having more people open more and bigger doors for you, far more of your marketing is on building relationships. That's wonderful news when your budget has limits. That's also wonderful news if you don't want to tweet or spend time on Facebook because you don't even enjoy it.

12. **It frees up time since you meet with warmer prospects that are much more likely to do business with you.** It is more productive than spending time with people who are not ready, indecisive, simply kicking tires, or price shopping.

13. **You get measurable results every time.** You know exactly where the business is coming from and where it's not coming from. This awareness allows you to focus on the relationships and organizations that are helping your business the most.

14. **You can feel more peace of mind being more recession-proof.** You have a business based on great relationships and people who recommend you to others.

Got Desire?

Your desire and attitude determine your success level. How you feel determines your actions. Your actions—what you do—determine your results.

The exciting part is that you are totally responsible for your results. How much you want more referrals is going to be the key. You wouldn't be reading this book if you weren't motivated at all. But how well you can motivate yourself to take a lot of action—that's truly up to you.

It's easy to talk a good game. While who you *are* as a person is most important, your truest values are revealed by what you actually *do*—by how you spend your time, not by what you say or have written down on a business plan.

How do you get more motivated to want more referrals?

Try Some Pain: Rule of 20 Percent–60 Percent–20 Percent

Based on two studies on the financial services industry in 2005 and published in Horsesmouth, LLC's *Automatic Referrals*, the research found that only 11 percent of clients had been asked for referrals. Yet 72 percent and 83 percent, respectively, of those surveyed said they would happily recommend their advisor but had not been asked. How many of your clients do you ask?

Most people get unsolicited referrals from about 20 percent of their clients—2 people in 10. Many salespeople fool themselves into thinking that they have a great referral business because of this 20 percent.

But I believe that there are another 6 in 10 (60 percent) of your clients who would endorse you but need to be asked, and you need to use Steps 3 and 5 from Chapter 6 so it is easy for them. They're not thinking about you until you ask. *How many of your clients do you ask?*

If the answer is none, then *how much more business do you think you could bring in if you effectively asked those 60 percent?* (It's important to note that you must earn the referral before you ask for it. We'll cover that in an upcoming chapter, so keep reading!)

It's also fair to say that there will usually be 1 or 2 in 10 (10 to 20 percent) who just aren't going to recommend you. Maybe they can be turned around in time, but they may well be unnecessary "projects."

TRY SOME PLEASURE

First, I suggest that you reread the 14 referral benefits from the previous section. Soak them up. Second, if your referral business is coming from 20 percent of your clients and you're hardly asking any of them, think about what your business would look like if another 6 in 10 (60 percent) of your clients were recommending you!

Not every referral is created equal. I am not going to claim you'll see a 300 percent increase in business. Ultimately, there will still likely be an 80–20 law in most cases (where you're getting 80 percent of your business from 20 percent of the people you know). But until you've asked everyone who is happy with your work (or is considered a "go-to" reference person or friend), what could that untapped potential be? And if a lot more people send you business, that 80–20 spread is going to be much higher up the scale from your present situation!

To get closer to where you want to be, set some exciting referral goals. Remember, it's what it makes of you that matters most, not what it makes for you. Why? Because it is who you become that matters most. You will stretch yourself and think bigger. Your confidence will grow from facing your fears.

These goals need not focus on money. For most people it's better if they don't. Focus on helping more people, on achieving results in other parts of your life, and on getting better at what you do in measurable ways. Good goals can simply be about implementing the Six-Step Fearless Referral Conversation (see Chapter 6).

When you set your goals, set the bar as high as you can. Author Tim Ferriss points out in his book *The 4-Hour Workweek* that you will have more success aiming higher for two reasons:

1. Ninety-nine percent of people are "convinced they are incapable of achieving great things" and so they never try. That means there are very few people going for gold. If everyone else feels insecure, you don't need to be the one selling yourself short.

2. When you do have an ambitious target, it gets your adrenaline going and you think of more creative solutions. *It's as easy as believing it can be done.*

While in England on a recent trip, I picked up David Lester's highly informative *How They Started: How 30 Good Ideas Became Great Businesses.*

In his introduction, Lester notes that almost everyone on the planet has an idea or two for a business; it's just that most people don't pursue that idea—and fewer still succeed. While those that succeeded all *behaved* in similar ways—it was how they went about growing their business that made the difference.

For most top entrepreneurs, at first there was little monetary reward. Many months and even years later, very little of the money they made was spent on themselves. Quite a few of the 30 people featured worked part time on their business until they thought they could take the leap.

They all focused on one idea. They all kept it simple. Yes, 18-hour days were pretty common because starting momentum takes a great deal of effort and commitment. "None of the founders started out as workaholics—they all began as normal people just like you."

But for each of them, the key was they kept trying and believing.

About half of the businesses in the book had weak sales early on and had to wait much longer than they expected for business to pick up. Every business Lester profiled "had to overcome significant issues to keep trading, let alone succeed; along the way, each founder faced doubt, anxiety, stress and pressure levels way beyond what most employees face; their ability to cope with this, almost always deeply rooted in strong self belief, was an important factor in why they succeeded where so many businesses haven't."

They had motivation, passion, and commitment. This is what you need to improve your referral business.

None of the business owners interviewed set out to become wealthy. *None of them!* Their motives ranged from wanting a livelihood after being laid off, to wanting to create a higher-quality product or service not then available, to wanting to see if they could make it in a new market.

Lester concludes that it wasn't about being from the right stock or wanting more money that drove these businesses to succeed. They had a focused idea for a product or service that some part of the world needed. "And they needed literally extraordinary levels of passion, energy, self-belief and stamina, the ability and desire to focus, and a good measure of judgment."

My final point here, and arguably the most important, is that your motivation comes most profoundly and lasts longer when tied to your sense of purpose—why you were put on this earth. Connecting to that will take you where you want to go. I sincerely wish you all a healthy dose of these qualities so that you get the referrals and the results you want!

IT'S A SKILL YOU CAN LEARN IF YOU HAVE A GROWTH MINDSET!

Ever catch yourself thinking about someone who gets more referrals than you and saying, "He's a natural," or "She's a lot smarter than I am," or "That person is so much more experienced than I am"?

Even worse, have you ever said, "I don't have that in me"?

Most of us have. Be assured: they have learned their skills somewhere along the line, and you can too—*but only if you believe that's within you!*

What we tend to do is put the "naturals" on a pedestal based on qualities they have that we think we don't have. For me, when I was newer to the business world, that person was Lorelle. Back then, I thought she had an innate "gift" for giving and getting referrals. She was very good at both—better than anyone else I knew.

I told myself that:

1. She had a more charming personality than I had.

2. She was more business savvy than I was.

3. She had the gift of gab.

4. She was better looking than I was.

It was the perfect storm of an excuse.

Looking back now, I can reflect differently. Lorelle had been in sales for more than 15 years compared to my 1 year. She was highly motivated (as was I) and had attended many more seminars and read dozens more books than I had. She had had a lot more time to practice what she had learned.

Personality and looks—yes, I thought she had both, but these are subjective qualities. Not everyone would have agreed. And why should the rest of us walk around as though we are inferior because we don't look like models? Look at the people who get your business— would they all look good parading on a catwalk? It's true that these things may impact some decisions, but they are not going to stop you from great success.

Getting good at referrals is a learnable business communication and relationship-building skill.

The only people who cannot acquire this skill are those who:

♦ Have weak relationships with others

♦ Are purely transactional

♦ Are never going to muster the courage or self-belief to ask for what they want

♦ Are unable to overcome concerns about asking

♦ Believe that business skill and intelligence are basic fixed things that can't be changed much

Let me explain that last one. Carol Dweck is a world-renowned psychologist at Stanford University. I saw her speak a few days ago in Chicago about her book *Mindset*. I learned much more about why some people don't get good at generating referrals.

Her decades of research have found that there are essentially two mindsets (fixed and growth) that people have about intelligence and other skills and talents (such as business, artistic, and sporting ability). *A mindset is a powerful belief.*

Which do you believe?

Your intelligence is something very basic about you that you can't change very much.

or

No matter how much intelligence you have, you can always change it quite a bit.

If I had a fixed mindset or belief about getting referrals, I could not have developed myself because I started out so badly. I'd have taken one look at Lorelle and either abandoned any hope of getting good at generating referrals, blamed my parents or teachers for not giving me the skills because they weren't in business or sales, or found a way to look superior to Lorelle ("I'm a better speaker and writer than she is—who cares about referrals!," etc.).

Luckily, a growth mindset or belief meant I was willing to struggle for a while, willing to work hard at getting better, and willing to take risks and fail from time to time.

The key word is *belief.* Since all our results come from our beliefs, Dweck tells us that we have to change our beliefs first. *If you believe that you might reveal your inadequacies by taking risks, experiencing initially weak results, and working hard, you won't do what is needed to get great results and build a referral-based business.* (And if your results are still poor in six months, read this again and read Dweck's book too!)

Fixed mindset. If I have to work hard, it makes me feel like I'm not smart.

Growth mindset. The harder I work, the better I get.

The fixed mindset is afraid of challenges and sees failure as making a mistake—revealing that you are not perfect and smart all the time. The growth mindset sees failure as growing (learning) and views struggle as part of that process. The good news is you can change your mindset. If you want to get better at generating referrals, you must have a growth mindset or you will not do the work.

I cannot emphasize how significant this is. Without a growth mindset, you will never be successful at bringing in more and better referrals.

DELIBERATE PRACTICE

According to the research reported in Geoff Colvin's recent *Talent Is Overrated*, top performers are generally *not*:

- **Naturally gifted.** Most of the people who became the most accomplished in their field "did not show early evidence of gifts."

- **Exclusively hard workers.** We all know people who work plenty of hours who achieve average results.

- **More experienced.** We all know people with more experience than we have who get average results.

- **Higher in IQ.** We all know people who are smarter than we are who get average results.

- **Born with great memories.** Do you get the point?

Believing any of these things simply gives people an excuse to be mediocre. The key message in this book is that superior performers pursue *deliberate practice* in areas that address specific skills that take them *around* their limitations.

This is what you need to do to get high-quality referrals on a consistent basis.

One great sports example is Jerry Rice, the former San Francisco 49er (since most of us have not been professional athletes, look for the concepts here). The records he holds are not 5 or 10 percent higher than the statistics for the person in second place (which would still be impressive), but 50 percent! He played 20 seasons—until he was 42—in a position where the average player does not make it to age 30. Yet he was not considered fast by professional standards.

Rice's success came "because he worked harder in practice and in the off-season than anyone else" and because *he designed his practice to work on his specific needs*. He focused intently on the four things he had to excel in to compensate for his lack of speed: the running of precise patterns (strength training), explosive acceleration (uphill wind sprints), endurance training for stamina late in games, and sudden changes in directions without signaling his intent (trail running).

His off-season training regimen was considered so brutal that his coaches refused to share it with anyone for fear that others might damage themselves!

It's not just graft that gets you places; it's the right kind of practice activity that can help you get better results. The same is true for getting more referrals. What are you doing to improve your game?

WHAT WILL MAKE ME BETTER AT WHAT I DO?

In general, do you need to practice in:

- Running your first appointments so they lead to more meetings?
- Making prospecting calls?
- Honing your referral conversation?
- Running effective center-of-influence meetings?

- Identifying better new referral prospects with your current contacts?
- Coaching others to refer you effectively?
- Giving more referrals?

Look at the results you get from asking for referrals (which is a specific skill you can practice). Could the people you ask be sending you more referrals? Do you need to:

- Increase your networking activities and coffees with potential centers of influence?
- Join someone you know who runs meetings well and learn from them?
- Change the wording that you use?
- Create a meeting agenda so you don't run out of time?

The only way to be more effective prospecting, getting referrals, or being a networker is to pinpoint your weaknesses and work around them. Learn more about what the most effective producers do.

SUPERIOR PERFORMERS PERCEIVE, KNOW, AND REMEMBER MORE

Superior performers notice things average performers do not. They look ahead for trends. They know more from seeing less. They are more expert in their field because they study more. Their ability to recall and interpret information is also superior. They see themselves as responsible for the things that do not go well; they are always getting better, and they are always overstraining themselves mentally.

Most of these things you can decide to start doing more of today too!

Getting There Is Tough but Is Available to Almost Anyone

The highest achievers in any field have accumulated many more life-time hours of practice than everyone else. Colvin calls it the "Ten-Year Rule" (10 years before you can become acclaimed), which is rather similar to what author and journalist Malcolm Gladwell has called the "10,000 Hour Rule." This is the dominant reason why so-called child prodigies appear to be innately talented. Tiger Woods's father had a metal golf club in his son's hands from the age of *seven months* and had him on a golf course at two years old! Mozart's father had his son on a program of intensive training in composing and performing at age three.

The Chief Constraint Is Mental

You won't make any progress if you work hard and then just do things in your comfort zone. You need to step outside your comfort zone regularly and face your fears.

University of Michigan business professor Noel Tichy has identified three areas where we spend our time mentally: the comfort zone (useless), the learning zone (great), and, beyond that, the panic zone (unproductive). To become top of your game, you must get in your learning zone as much as possible "and then force yourself] to stay continuously in it as it changes, which is even harder—these are the first and most important characteristics of deliberate practice."

The great mental intangible to sustaining this is your motivation. Colvin reports that most researchers believe that this drive must be primarily *intrinsic* because of the sacrifices necessary to be the best. It is founded in people's desire to solve a great question or problem in their field (enjoying their focus on the process, not the outcome or goal), to do good in the world, to make progress, to be the best, to be an achiever or desire power.

A great example of this is that most eminent executives and entrepreneurs keep working long after they need to. What do you think was the first thing Bill Cosby did when he sold the rights to *The Cosby Show* for $250 million? Take a month off and sit on the beach? Party in Paris? No, he took a red-eye flight to Vegas so he could test out some new material in a stand-up routine for his next project.

When is extrinsic motivation effective? At times, recognition and feedback can really help, provided that the feedback is constructive, nonthreatening, and work-focused—rather than person-focused.

WHAT DO YOU WANT?

Much of this boils down to what you want in life, what you believe you're capable of doing, and whether you believe your work will pay off. Passion develops over time based on how much action you take (not on waiting for something to happen). The "eureka" moment of a genius idea is mostly a myth and generally comes after years of intensive preparation.

SUPPORT, FEEDBACK, REPETITION, AND ACTIVITY DESIGNED TO IMPROVE PERFORMANCE

Especially at critical times in a person's development, Colvin recommends the importance of an outside eye to see the things you cannot see about yourself.

"It's apparent why becoming significantly good at almost anything is extremely difficult without the help of a teacher or coach, at least in the early going." He says there's a reason why the best golfers still work with coaches. (See Chapter 7 on the team you need to get you to the top.) A supportive environment matters.

Last, Colvin does say that *nothing* can fully explain achievement because "real life is too complicated for that." However, clearly there is much that can be done by each of us to move from beyond being average to aiming to make more of a difference and ultimately becoming one of the best in our field. Getting better at bringing in more referrals is a great place to focus.

The Three "Musts" for Me to Help You

For you to get the most out of this book, here are three things I urge you to do.

Don't Reinvent the Wheel

As humans, we innately believe we can and should come up with our own solutions. The challenging reality is that this belief is often false. Unfortunately, we overestimate our abilities and do not realize that we are average at most things. Harvard psychology professor Daniel Gilbert's research is just one recent example of social science finding that we do a *terrible* job of evaluating ourselves: we typically overrate our abilities and underestimate our knowledge. We tend to seek out information that already supports what we believe, and we tend to discount information that contradicts it!

The statistics are quite hilarious. For example, one study found that 90 percent of drivers consider themselves to be safer than average. In regard to college professors, 94 percent consider themselves to be above-average educators. However, only 50 percent can actually be above average and the other 50 percent below average.

We rely on our own (flawed) memory and imagination rather than follow those who have been there and done it. *We are more likely to make our own mistakes rather than learn from those who have already made them.* You do not need to do that with getting referrals. Because we see ourselves as unique, we often think that the experiences of others do not apply to us. Most of the time, this is not true.

What does this all mean? It means you need to work harder—but it's equally important to follow the suggestions in this book because they work. Don't try to reinvent the wheel. The content of this book has been tried and tested over many years with thousands of people. Don't resist implementing ideas that work for others. The very fact that others have done it is proof you can do it too—not proof you should buck the trend because that's how you live your life.

However, do make these ideas your own!

Tweak them to fit your personality and communication style. If you read an example and say to yourself, "I would never say that!" then pause and ask yourself how you might reword it to make the same point.

BE COACHABLE

I'm guessing you wouldn't have picked up this book if you weren't open to new ideas. However, you'll only be able to successfully increase your referral business if you act on new ideas. Your key to gaining referrals is action, persistence, and belief. Avoid just "trying" something once and then convincing yourself that it doesn't work. It just takes discipline.

Very few people are willing to (1) customize content to make it suit your personality, (2) be open-minded to some new ideas, and (3) persist—because it may not all happen overnight.

Being coachable isn't as easy as you might hope. Most salespeople and business owners pride themselves on their independence, and this often includes the notion that they can figure pretty much everything out themselves. This is a strong quality, and it will take you to good, even to above average, but it will not take you to great. I did not see this in my life until relatively recently. Then I opened my eyes and realized that all high achievers reach out for support, guidance, and (often) coaching. It is not a coincidence that all top performers—golfers, cyclists, writers, speakers—work with qualified coaches.

I just ask that you be aware that as you read this, you're not out to prove that parts of this can't work for you because you're different or your business is different. *Getting referrals is not that complicated, and if you think it is, that may well be your defense mechanism to keep success away from you.* (You might want to read that again.)

Finally, if what you're doing right now works really well for you, then keep doing it if it's ethical. If you're a manager and you want to train others to do the same, go ahead *provided it works as well for them*! That's a big caveat because often things don't translate so well.

PERSIST

Numbers rarely lie. A study I found in Jack Canfield's *The Success Principles* shares work done by Herbert True at Notre Dame that demonstrates how incredibly important it is simply never to give up.

His research of salespeople found that:

- 44 percent gave up after one request to do business.
- 68 percent had given up after two requests or less.
- 82 percent gave up after three requests or less.
- 94 percent gave up after four requests or less.

If 94 percent of them gave up after asking four times for the business, then only 6 percent really persisted. Just 6 percent! But here's the really dramatic part: *60 percent of all sales are made after the fourth call.*

Is it any wonder that the top 6 percent of salespeople make so much more money than the rest?

MORE FRIENDS = MORE REFERRALS: MASTER THE LIKEABILITY FACTOR AND THE COMFORT FACTOR

Last summer I was in Canada having lunch with my cousin, the owner of a fairly novel branding and design business called Breakhouse. He, an interior designer, and his business partner, an architect, turn retail stores into a "Starbucks-type experience" and tie that experience into the new company brand. He was telling me that they had recently landed their biggest client to date: Bell Canada, the Canadian equivalent of AT&T or British Telecom. Apparently Bell Canada's retail sales had dropped from first to third in the country, and so the company was working on a new corporate image.

My favorite question to ask people is to trace how they got the business. He explained that they had worked with a local telecom company in eastern Canada and this work had won an award. The company referred them to Bell Canada. That's right, Breakhouse doesn't advertise. All Breakhouse's business comes from referrals.

Three other companies were vying for the business: Goliaths by comparison—two from New York and one from the Netherlands. Two of these other companies have 500 employees each; the other has an international client list to die for. "So how did you beat these guys out?" I had to know. I don't want to oversimplify my point. He cited two or three reasons. Their proposal was impressive, and he was pretty sure they had put more effort into it than their competitors. They were Canadian; he wasn't sure if that had helped or not. "But you know what I think it was? I think they just liked us more. My business partner is a pretty funny guy. He's good at connecting with people and loosening them up. We just hit it off."

This reminds me of a coffee I had with a mortgage consultant that I've known for about six years. She used to network everywhere and was excellent at both giving and asking for referrals. I know

I learned some things from her. Then 10 months before I saw her, she became pregnant. Due to her diabetes, she was unable to drive for eight months. Her face-to-face networking abruptly stopped. Yet she was still getting a lot of referrals coming in. When I asked her what she was doing to maintain relationships, she told me. It was the same kind of stuff every mortgage professional I've ever met does: send out rate updates and help prepare flyers for open houses. I was really puzzled. This activity was not setting her apart at all.

Then it clicked. What she has is the Likeability Factor—the L-Factor. She treats people like they are her best friends. She has mastered how to be genuinely pleased to see you. You can see it on her face, and you can hear it in her voice on the phone. It is sincere, and while it sounds like common sense, we know this is rare. Think about it for a moment: who do you know who does this consistently? She knows how people want to be treated, and she does it even when she doesn't feel like it. This had helped her sustain her success.

It's not that we don't already know all this; the question is, why don't we run our businesses based on the L-Factor all the time? Why do we sometimes prospect people we don't much care for and who treat us like vermin? Do you focus your prospecting and client retention efforts on your top 20 percent—the ones who will inevitably refer you the most?

WHAT IS THE L-FACTOR?

Former Yahoo! executive Tim Sanders wrote *The Likeability Factor* in 2005, and it is full of research that supports the feeling we all have that people want to do business with and associate with others they know, like, and trust. These are the people we want to refer. Again, what are you doing about it? (In his book *The Little Red Book of Selling*, sales guru Jeffrey Gitomer gives this advice: "Win sales based on friendship, not price. Be friendly first.")

BE REAL

Others call this authenticity. Sanders argues that people need to be able to read your feelings. Failing to connect can make it difficult to get a business relationship off the ground—and you will get fewer referrals as a result. People will go to bat for you more when they really like you.

FOUR OUTSTANDING TIPS ABOUT THE L-FACTOR WORTH SHARING

These tips are from Jeffrey Gitomer's *The Little Red Book of Selling*. Read this list more than once and live it!

1. **"I put value in the hands of my potential customers before I ever ask them to buy anything."** Anyone who has heard me present or been coached by me hears me emphasize this point over and over. Bring as much value to a client meeting up front regardless of whether it has anything to do with your business. It will set you apart very quickly. Why? Because it shows you care, it takes a little effort, and most people won't take the time.

2. **Make friends before you start, or don't start.** Business gets so much easier when there is water in the well with a relationship. Any time another person can feel a connection with you, you have the advantage over other companies and their marketing techniques.

3. **Act professionally; speak friendly.** Gitomer has made me realize that sometimes I am too stiff because somehow I think it will raise my credibility and that I do not always focus on the L-Factor. Instead I run the risk of being seen as a cardboard box. Gitomer notes, "I try to act as professionally as I can, but I always err on the side of being too friendly." This also allows him to ask for a higher price and get it.

Another thought: I like to get down to business because I know people are busy. This practice, though, overlooks the people who want to "connect" first, and I risk losing that business.

I learned an interesting point from Britain's best-known magician, Paul Daniels. He observed in an interview that real experts are "light" with their subject matter and don't feel the need to take themselves too seriously. This takes time to develop. He's not suggesting such people don't speak with eloquence and earnestness. I think he's saying that they don't live in fear that one day they are going to get "found out" as not really being credible. They are comfortable in their own skin.

4. **If you make a sale, you earn a commission. If you make a friend, you can earn a fortune.** While you always want to be doing business for the right reasons and in the other person's best interests, many of the relationships you have can grow into friendships. The knock-on effects multiply as you have more fun in your work. This makes you more referable and more of a magnet for new business.

More Friends = More Referrals!

Here are four final thoughts on the relationship between friendship and referrals:

1. **The wildly underestimated Comfort Factor.** Author Harry Beckwith, a renowned expert on brand positioning and corporate branding strategies, has conducted much research on the Comfort Factor. In his enormously helpful book (coauthored with Christine Clifford-Beckwith), *You, Inc.*, he determined that when it comes to finding the best of the best, people do not really know what the best company is for any industry. No one

can be sure that his or her service providers are necessarily the best—it's very subjective.

Who can say which car or brand of jeans is the best on the market? Can you look others in the eye and tell them your veterinarian or Realtor is without doubt the best in the country?

Why do people continue to do business with personal service firms? According to Beckwith, "Their answer is one word. You hear this word from clients more than all their words combined. The word is *comfort*.

We work with people who make us feel comfortable.

2. **The law of attraction.** According to Gallup research, 99 percent of people would rather spend time with positive people who make them feel good. Typically if you don't like yourself all that much, you are unlikely to attract many others because you will not be instilling confidence in them. Both Jack Canfield and Nathaniel Brandon have terrific resources on this topic, which you'll find listed in the bibliography.

3. **Compassion.** Two weeks ago I was having a beer with my friend Gabe. He is a financial advisor in Tennessee. He told me two stories of people for whom he'd made a huge difference by asking them difficult questions that helped them get clear about major life decisions—adoption and career change.

    On both occasions he shelved his own meeting agenda and sales goals to listen to their more pressing needs. His compassion ultimately helped both people make significant changes. His compassion created two raving fans, two people who became much bigger clients than he anticipated and two new referral sources.

4. **Enthusiasm for what you do.** How can you expect referrals if you have little real enthusiasm for what you're doing? One of my favorite sayings is you have two choices in life if you don't like

something: change what you're doing, or change how you look at it. To get fired up about what you do, it often revolves around helping others and making a difference. How do you do that, and is it fulfilling enough? You spend so many hours working that it is crucial you enjoy what you do.

More Friends = More Referrals: The Rule of Liking

Arizona State professor Robert Cialdini has been studying the field of social influence for more than 35 years. The Rule of Liking is one of his six universal principles. In his 1984 classic, *Influence: The Psychology of Persuasion*, he talks about Joe Girard, considered the "greatest car salesman" by the *Guinness Book of World Records*. He sold five cars or trucks *every day he worked*. When asked how this happened, Girard simply said that people had found someone they liked to buy from and a fair price.

From a referral standpoint, the question to ask yourself is, "How can I most add value to this person?" This truly is pivotal because the rule states that the more people like us, the more they want to help us.

Cialdini found five areas that often help us be better liked by others.

Physical Attractiveness

He cites studies from the political, legal, human resources, and educational fields that indicate startling findings: we often vote for the candidate we find more attractive, we often hire the people we find more attractive, lighter sentences and more favorable verdicts for damages are awarded to more attractive people, and schoolteachers are more lenient with more attractive students.

I know that *you* certainly wouldn't let such a thing influence you! Cialdini argues these things often happen unconsciously and automatically.

OK, you don't need to have plastic surgery, but at least think hard about your health habits and dress code. When others see that you take care of yourself, it can only be a positive contrast to those who do not. In one of his excellent audio programs, Brian Tracy notes that he was shocked when he realized that many of the triathlon and marathon runners he knew were also the highest achievers in their fields.

SIMILARITY

Since most of us are average looking (not you, of course—you're in the top 10 percent, right?), there is still hope: *We like people who are similar to us.* This can vary from opinions, personalities, background, lifestyle, age, religion, politics, and the way we dress to seemingly trivial similarities, such as the rock bands we liked when we were 14.

John H. Johnson, who was born in a tin-roof shack in Arkansas in 1918, was the founder of *Ebony* magazine and the first black American on the *Forbes* magazine list of the 400 richest people in the United States. Whenever he was to meet someone for the first time, he would do his research to find a similarity: "I want to know where they came from, what are their interests, what can I talk to them about. You have to establish rapport with people, and you establish rapport by having mutual interests and mutual knowledge of each other."

It is very difficult to sell anything to someone if you have no common ground.

DO IT!

For the rest of this week, add one new question to each meeting that helps you learn something personal about the person you are meeting with—hometown, family, favorite team, how the person got started in his or her profession.

COMPLIMENTS

So what else did Joe Girard do to make such remarkable sales? He sent greeting cards *every month* to the 13,000-plus people in his network. Inside the card were three words: "I like you," and his signature.

Now, this was the 1970s, and if you're like me, you're thinking "That's so corny and transparent." Cialdini believes otherwise: "Joe understands an important fact about human nature: we are phenomenal suckers for flattery."

No, not false praise, but it is time to ask yourself how often you say nice things to others and how often you are keeping in touch with your clients in a way that makes *them* feel good.

CONTACT AND COOPERATION

Frequent contact is essential. We do not realize how much we are influenced by exposure to something on a repeated basis—this is why you will get more business (including referrals) from people if you keep your name in front of them year-round.

Cooperating with others on a common project or for a specific cause can be a powerful reason for liking. This is supported by Thomas J. Stanley's research discussed in *Networking with Millionaires*: "People see you at your best when you are doing something for a charitable cause." You are so much more likely to make deeper connections by meeting people when doing nonprofit work or by participating in the same professional association than by meeting someone at a business after hours because you have more commitment invested in the same project. These deeper bonds are more likely to lead to referral relationships.

I recently saw a high-producing financial advisor from Boston speak, and he said that every month he would identify the 25 people who had the biggest impact on his business. The last time he had done this he had found that 17 of them were people he had met through his volunteer work with the Make-a-Wish Foundation.

NEGATIVE AND POSITIVE ASSOCIATION

Not surprisingly, you'll want to avoid *negative association*. You've heard the phrase "kill the messenger." After years of poking fun at meteorologists, I had no idea that it was not unusual for them to receive hate mail—and worse—because of their predictions. People have blamed them for spoiling travel plans, crops, basements, weddings, and almost everything else under the sun.

On the other hand, *positive association* is a plus. This is why products use celebrities to endorse them—sales increase; it's why products call themselves the "official" hair spray, or deodorant, or checking account, of the U.S. Olympic Team or any other well-regarded event or organization. Irrationally, the product has more credibility, and so we like it more. It's why companies use attractive models to enhance what they're selling.

Two other interesting revelations:

1. Politicians and fund-raisers know that people will approve of you more (and give you more money) after you have fed them a nice meal. Feeding people can boost likeability.

2.   Some people are fanatical about their favorite sports teams; sharing a love for the same team can boost your Likeability Factor. Somehow, that team starts to represent you and prove your superiority—when the team wins. It is highly amusing to note that most people say the following after a game:

When your team wins, you say, "*We* won!"
When your team loses, you say, "*They* lost."

This is one reason why it is always wise to speak positively and optimistically about your business or company. Other people want to associate with winners.

As a reminder: for more referrals, the question to ask yourself is, "How can I most add value to this person?" Use the ideas just mentioned, because the more people like you, the more they want to help you.

CHAPTER 2

Earning the Fearless Referral

Our only real economic security lies in our power to meet human needs; (it) does not lie in our organizations or our jobs.

—Stephen Covey, *The 8th Habit*

◆

Before you start asking clients for referrals, there are some rules you need to consider.

You Only Ask for Referrals If You've Earned Them!

Too much of what we hear about referrals is based on techniques: how to ask, when to ask, what to say, and whom to get them from. We don't spend enough time focusing on *what* we are actually doing to earn the word-of-mouth recommendation.

Let's look at some word-of-mouth facts highlighted in Andy Sernovitz's *Word of Mouth Marketing*:

PEOPLE DON'T TALK ABOUT THE ORDINARY

Have you ever recommended that someone eat at Perkins or Burger King? Pizza Hut? Ever told friends they should try Coca-Cola? No. It's too ordinary.

How do your clients see you? Is it possible many of your clients see you as business as usual? Most salespeople will say no to this—after all, none of us thinks we are ordinary. But how often do you walk out of a business, or store, or restaurant, saying to yourself, "That place had really good service!"? Not very often, right? Are you *sure* you're that much better and provide significantly better service than your competition?

WHEN PEOPLE'S EXPECTATIONS ARE MET, THEY DO *NOT* TALK ABOUT IT TO OTHERS

When you go to the dentist, you expect him or her to take care of your teeth. When you take your sick dog to the vet, you expect your dog to get well. If you hire someone to service your air conditioner, you expect it to run better after that person leaves.

My point? Simply doing your job isn't enough. You must exceed expectations. We don't apply this thinking to our own clients and our own business enough.

Because our brains are wired to think about ourselves 95 percent of the time, we somehow assume that our service is better than everyone else's—even if it isn't. At almost every networking event I've ever been to, someone earnestly tells me that the unique part of his business is the customer service. This gets pretty meaningless after a while.

If you really want more referrals, you must truly *exceed* expectations.

It's More Important to Be Different Than It Is to Be Better

People don't just talk about what's best; they talk about what's different. Here are a few examples:

Jeffrey Gitomer has branded himself as the top sales authority in the United States. Is he really? His content is very good, and he's branded himself marvelously as different—funny, creative, not a "suit." It seems to resonate well with people.

Is Larry Winget really one of the best motivational speakers in the United States? He dresses like a biker. He looks different from all his competition. He has successfully branded himself as an in-your-face type of guy. He knows his stuff. Does he know more than anyone else?

John Eliot is a professor at Rice University who writes and speaks on peak performance. He has branded himself differently not by his appearance or marketing savvy, but by his opinions and the way he states them to catch people's attention: goal setting is for couch potatoes; hard work is overrated; stress is a good thing. It got me to read his book *Overachievement* (once I saw his credentials), and it is full of great research and ideas.

Yes, these people are all good, but what makes them stand out is what makes them different. Differentiating yourself doesn't have to be world changing. It could be making an initially powerful impact when people first walk into your place of business. Some banks and car dealerships now have Starbucks machines in them. That was once a wow factor.

Perhaps you differentiate yourself through providing excellent follow-up and keeping in touch. Trent, a Realtor I know well, does this better than anyone else I've ever met. Think about how many people want your business but fail to show they care about you since they don't keep in touch. I got one e-mail after I spent almost $40,000 on a car a year or so ago. Not even a call. I've bought three properties in my lifetime. Only one of the Realtors I worked with kept in regular contact. Would you refer someone who didn't even follow up to say thank you?

IT'S CUSTOMER SURPRISES, NOT CUSTOMER SERVICES, THAT COUNT

I say this to emphasize that "business as usual" nets zero referrals. Great customer service matters greatly, but what people remember most are the nice surprises. Last weekend I opened my mailbox to find that someone who had been to a recent seminar of mine had sent me a book. (This is a very quick way to win my heart!) And it wasn't a book about her business; it wasn't some vague ruse to sell me something. On the contrary, it was a book she knew I would really want to read. Every time I see that book, I remember who gave it to me. Bottles of wine are nice, but they get consumed quickly. That book will be a permanent reference tool for me.

Here are other real-life examples of people I've worked with as referral coaching clients or met at seminars who earn many referrals:

♦ An insurance agent who takes one weekend a year and makes quilts for the clients who have the most policies with her

♦ Two mortgage consultants who offer you water, coffee, or *beer* when you arrive (and mean it!)

♦ An insurance agent who has a community notice board where locals can advertise for a babysitter, sell a boat, or promote a yard sale

♦ A Realtor who routinely gives away fresh eggs, homemade jam, and just-made maple syrup

♦ A financial advisor who regularly invites his best clients to Red Sox, Patriots, and Celtics games

Keep Filling Up the Wells with Water

Referrals do not come out of thin air or thin relationships: You can't get water out of an empty well.

Get Your Clients Talking about Their Passions

George Silverman, former president of the Word of Mouth Marketing Association, said, "People talk about their passions. You can't get them to shut up about their passions."

Think about yourself here. You love talking about your kids, your favorite team, a hobby, your pet, a favorite band, or a vacation destination. *Your clients like you more when they know you care enough to ask them about theirs.*

One of the reasons I like my vet so much is that he is one of the few people outside my family who *sincerely* asks me about what I care about most: my wife and family, my business, and my dog, Scooby. Kurt, one of my past clients, always used to ask me about Coventry City, my hometown team, even though it rarely feels good to talk about them because they are pretty awful! I still appreciated him remembering.

Maybe your clients are not that interested in what you do professionally, just as you may not be very interested in what they *do*. So know what they do care about most and talk to them about that!

Actually, better than getting your clients to talk about their passions is when you can help them to connect more to what they love.

Do we all know exactly what we want in life? Do we have all the time we want to connect to our passions? Here are some ways to help your clients reconnect with their passions.

Host Client Events That Revolve around Something Your Clients Love

Bring people together who have the same strong interests in life. They will talk to each other, and you will initiate great word of mouth about you! That's one reason why target marketing works so well (all people with a common interest).

Here are some examples of successful client events:

♦   A friend of mine who owns a business has several events each year at Green Bay Packers and Milwaukee Brewers games.

♦   A friend of mine who is a florist hosts a variety of events on gardening, interior design, creative gift ideas, and floral design followed by a 15 percent discount off everything in the store before customers leave.

♦   A former client of mine who is a financial advisor has hosted events at a microbrewery where clients and guests get a tour and great beer-tasting experience. How easy do you suppose it is for his clients to invite friends to that!

Be a Resource to Your Clients

Do you know the best resources in town who may be able to help your clients? The more people you know professionally who have different specialties, the more you can become a resource to your clients. (Additionally, by referring others, they are much more likely, in turn, to refer you—my next book will address how to master this.) This is a way to position yourself as a "go-to" person and build trust with clients.

Almost everyone has money worries at times—do you know people who can help your clients in those areas? Know a good travel agent or travel Web site for your client wanting to get away in the winter? Know a massage therapist for your stressed client? How about a friend who has connections to get tickets for sporting events or knows about the best plays or bands coming to town? The list is endless. Create more traffic through you. Create more buzz. Very few professionals have that reputation—why not be that person? It's word of mouth, remember?

You can make a huge difference for people you know.

HELP OTHERS GET WHAT THEY WANT FIRST

When you help others get what they want first, asking for referrals gets a whole lot easier. This just might be the most important statement in the book! I know this has almost become a cliché, but like most clichés it's founded on a great deal of truth. Maybe nobody has ever done any scientific research on it, but it surely seems that the more you give to others, the more you get.

The more you go above and beyond with a client, the more business you get. The more you help a center of influence, the more business comes back to you.

It's not always tit for tat, and you certainly don't want to keep score. You might send three pieces of business to one professional and help someone at a networking event find a job. You might not receive anything specific from these people, but perhaps you'll get all kinds of opportunities from others.

HUMAN RESEARCH

Why do we hear so much about helping others and yet often find it hard to do? It is counterintuitive. Research has shown that humans are innately wired to focus on their own needs 95 percent of the time. If you're spending 95 percent of your time focused on getting referrals, that's great. The only problem is that you really need to spend more than 5 percent of your time thinking about how you can help others. It also means that the people you want referrals from are not thinking about you!

Three years ago, I met a lawyer who had brought in $1.1 million of new business to his firm in 2006. He attributed it almost entirely to the fact that he had referred so much business to others. He did a lot of giving, and he didn't keep score about who gave back. He just knew that creating that much goodwill would make good things happen.

Help Others Succeed

You will often have to help others succeed first—or at least try. And you'll need to keep helping them. With clients this means continually taking care of their needs as well as you can and listening for other ways to make an impact. With centers of influence—other key professionals in your network who have a similar target market—it means a lot more.

Start a New Action Habit

Schedule time to add value to centers of influence and key clients. This will start a new mental habit of putting the needs of centers of influence high on your priority list.

This is not easy to do, and for most sales professionals, it does not come naturally. It takes practice, and it needs to be drilled into your head.

I don't know how many times I had to hear that before it truly sank in—I think for me it took about four years. That's how hard it was to stop focusing only on immediate business. The sooner you do it, the better.

I recently asked Adam, an insurance agent and past client of mine, why he was the only agent in his office to have referral partners. Look for his reasons:

> *My first question used to be "what's in it for me?" "How can he help me?" I wasn't thinking long term; I was only thinking about myself. I really needed a mindset shift. I had to trust you, as my referral coach, that it would be worth my while. And Tim [a former agent in his office] had had great success getting referrals from other professionals, and he had worked with you, so I knew it was possible; and he spoke really highly of you. I had no idea back then how great it could be.*

Six reasons! It took six different contributing factors before Adam was ready to do something. Now because Adam has done such a good job referring business to other professionals, he is a Presidents' Club qualifier in his company, 70 percent of his business comes from referrals, and 80 percent of that business comes from centers of influence.

I took a week off recently and returned to reading one of my favorite authors, Stephen Covey. This quotation grabbed me by the jugular so much that I had to read and reread it several times. It is from his book *First Things First*:

> *We settle for the illusion society sells us that meaning is in self-focus—self-esteem, self-improvement. But the wisdom literature of thousands of years repeatedly validates the reality that the greatest fulfillment in improving ourselves comes in our empowerment to more effectively reach out and help others. Quality of life is inside out. Meaning is in contribution, in living for something higher than self.*

Too often I get caught in the trap of thinking too egotistically about "what can I do that will help me and quick-fix cheer me up?" and wind up missing the point that I feel best when I'm helping others grow their business by getting more referrals, or coaching kids improv comedy on a Tuesday night, or spending time with friends and family, or playing with my sister's children, who are five and seven.

This is the kind of paradigm shift that could change everything for you. Happiness is not in the "me, me, me," but in making a difference to others. And that's where the referrals come, too!

UNDERSTAND AND APPLY THE RULE OF RECIPROCATION

For the past nine years I've listened to audio programs extolling the importance of bringing something to the table, of adding value first. Recently, author Bob Burg published a book titled *The Go-Giver*, which shares the compelling message of helping others. The idea is virtually a cliché!

There were times when this drove me nuts as I thought to myself, "I can't spend my time doling out free advice and helping others with their causes—I've got a business to run!" At times it sounded fluffy and new age. I felt like saying, "Yeah, easy for you to say, Mr. Millionaire International Speaker! I've got a growing relationship with my credit card company!" So here's what you need to understand as soon as possible: *the reason why helping other people is so highly recommended is because people often feel obligated to return the favor!* Read that again! It's the Rule of Reciprocation. Nobody had ever explained this to me before.

I knew deep down it made some sense, but taking the leap of faith was difficult for me. Now that I've read the psychology research, it makes sense. Cialdini first wrote about this in *Influence:*

The Psychology of Persuasion. He makes it clear that it is innate to humans that we feel we must help someone in return *provided the help the person gave us was genuine and unconditional.* (If we sense it's a scheme of sorts, it won't work.)

He notes that when we need to persuade and influence others, we mistakenly ask ourselves, "Who can help me here?" This approach rarely works because it comes off as needy—rather like saying, "I really need your help growing my business. Can you please, please refer me to everyone you know?" No! In Cialdini's latest book (written with coauthors Noah Goldstein and Steve J. Martin), called *Yes! 50 Secrets from the Science of Persuasion,* he advises: "It would be more productive to ask ourselves the question 'whom can I help?,' knowing that the norm of reciprocation and the social obligation it confers on others will make future requests more effective."

This is why it's vital to know what value you've brought to your clients before asking them for referrals (Step 2 of the Six-Step Fearless Referral Conversation; see Chapter 6). Have you helped them enough to earn a referral?

BOUNDARIES

You teach people how to treat you. You need to have boundaries in your business week about whom you help, and keep in mind that it may be a while before the favor is returned. I hate to sound calculating, but you are growing a business, not a nonprofit organization. Absolutely there are times to help others who are reaching out to you; mentoring others is incredibly rewarding. But most people don't have the time or money to randomly help everyone who knocks on their door. Does that person you're helping know others who might make good clients for you?

A friend of mine in the financial services industry developed a huge network and became known as a great resource for helping people between jobs. The problem is that somewhere along the line, people met with her expecting free advice and were not interested in discussing their financial situation and potential retirement rollover money with her. After some time, my friend simply grew resentful at not being appreciated.

Interestingly, this is where I find that the universal principle of how much you like the other person makes a big difference in how much you are willing to help!

Two Things to Think About

There are two things to consider if you want a *big* return from helping others.

What You Give Influences What You Get

The more a person gives to us, the more obligated we feel to give in return. Is your lightbulb on now? The more you sincerely help someone out, the more that person will feel obligated to help you in some way. Think about it. The last time you met someone for coffee or lunch and he or she picked up the tab; what was the first thought you had? Next time we get together, I better pay—I don't want to feel like a moocher! Or what about the last time someone helped you move to a new house? I am sure you did something to show your appreciation because the person really helped you out.

Gifts and Favors Are Most Persuasive

Three factors will determine to what degree these offerings are effective:

1. **The offering needs to be seen by the recipient as significant or meaningful.** I remember a financial advisor friend of mine was telling me that she was disappointed by the lack of response she had received after sending some of her clients subscriptions to *National*

Geographic. She had wanted to send something of value that both spouses might like. Unfortunately, the magazine evidently did not mean enough to those who got it. That's because of the next point.

2. **The offering needs to be personalized.** What are you most interested in? What would you remove from your mailbox and say, "This is great!"? What are your primary needs right now?

     I was in England three summers ago speaking to an organization about networking. Afterward, someone told me about some business that took four years to come her way. But during that time she had met the needs of her prospect several times by recommending writers to her (which was her prospect's primary need during this period).

3. **Unexpected is best.** This supports research done by Harvard psychologist Daniel Gilbert and by Gallup. I cannot recommend this idea more highly. I have had tremendous success surprising people with small gifts. Remember, it has to be sincere!

     Last year, on two different occasions, sales managers who had brought me in to present to their teams stood up during this point in my seminar and explained to their salespeople that they had decided to select me after unexpectedly receiving a book from me.

DO IT!

Identify the top 20 people in your network. For each person, decide: how can I most add value to this person? Give your brain a chance to come up with good ideas. Start putting more water in the well. My current client, Jason, sent out 16 copies of an inspiring book to some of his best contacts in the past month. Eight have thanked him already. The one referral he has received has already landed him a client worth $6 million.

MAKE EMOTIONAL BANK ACCOUNT DEPOSITS

One of the fundamental principles to getting referrals is *you can't get water out of an empty well*. You can't ask for anything if you haven't been adding value, making "deposits," and filling up the well yourself first. But what you add must have real value. You wouldn't readily recommend anything if it hadn't really done anything good for you. Your integrity is on the line.

Stephen Covey coined the phrase *emotional bank account*. His concept was that you can't have a strong relationship without constantly feeding it positive deposits. When you are adding to it on a regular basis, then there can be some give and take. If you ignore building it the right way, you can't expect anything in return. The same is true for referrals.

The last time I bought a new car, I got a call from the company asking me if I would recommend the dealership to friends and family. Over the phone I said I would because my experience had been very positive. But after I hung up, I concluded that I would hesitate to give a referral. I was trying to understand why I wouldn't recommend the company. I thought about it and realized that the car had to deliver for a while. I've had some bad experiences with cars, and I realized that I wouldn't recommend one until I knew it was coming through for me.

So far one good deposit has been made, but in this instance I will need many more before I would suggest someone else go there. For example, the salesperson who helped me didn't really seem very interested in me and what I did for a living (which strikes me as really strange since he could have fished for some free advice!). He earned the referral on his competence, but he did little to build the relationship.

I remember meeting someone at a business happy hour once. I barely spoke to him, didn't connect with him on a personal level when we did talk, and then was amazed when he started leaving me messages asking me to introduce his wife (whom I'd never met) to all my contacts in a specific industry! No deposits had been made, and yet he was asking me to risk my reputation for a total stranger. It's an extreme example, but it reminds us that we need to track the balance of lifting or leaning on a relationship.

How You Can Apply This Knowledge to Get More Referrals

Here are five things you can do to take what you know and use it to improve your referral rate:

1. **Find out how you've helped your clients.** This is discussed in detail in Chapter 6. Helping clients to realize fully how much you have helped them and *acknowledge what you have done for them recently* solidifies part one of the Rule of Reciprocation. You will hear whether you have made enough deposits and have earned the referral. If your client tells you that you have brought value, it makes transitioning to what you and I call a referral conversation that much easier.

2. **Keep regularly adding value to clients, referral partners, and potential centers of influence without expecting any immediate return.** This is something you can do every week. And you should do it regularly, so that your top 20 percent of contacts know that you have done something for them recently! Please, schedule it now! Make it a regular habit in your business week. Then the only question you need to answer is, "How can I most add value to this person?"

3. **Send items of value to your client base to keep you top of mind.** This could include free helpful information that is not selling something and that your clients might actually want to read—not pitch in the recycling bin. Perhaps articles or books

on topics that interest them, such as antique cars, hiking, or other hobbies, would be appreciated.

4. **Hold a client appreciation event.** There are many variations and possibilities here that can benefit the Rule of Reciprocation.

5. **Send luxury gifts at holiday time.** My friend Curt runs a software company, and he sends out high-quality wines, cigars, and chocolates during the holidays that are highly appreciated by his clients. He always has new business pouring in—not just in January. Be aware, though, that some companies have policies forbidding them to accept gifts for fear it will be perceived as a kickback from a vendor or as a bribe.

Master suggestions 2, 3, and 4 because these are the founding principles that govern the relationships you need to get a lot of referrals.

FIRST BE COMPETENT AND JARGON-FREE

Often I like to ask audiences about the people to whom they have referred business. I ask them to think about the qualities of the people they recommend to loved ones. There are only about five or six qualities that come up consistently. Competence is always one of them.

Nobody will recommend you if you are shaky on your subject matter. This is the first area you must be strong in as quickly as possible. There's a reason why every book on success talks about being a lifelong learner. Knowledge builds trust. As I write this today, I have just come from doing two presentations that were attended by a mere 5 percent of the association's invited membership—only 5 percent. Few people are committed to continuous self-improvement, and yet that's exactly what our clients want from us and that's exactly what will help you avoid being downsized.

I cannot say that the best informed person always runs the strongest business. Knowledge is not the only skill. Knowledge is only meaningful when you use it. But I can say that your knowledge base can only help you *and* that lack of competence will hurt you and damage your credibility and authenticity.

JUST STARTING OUT

How do you handle the problem of competency if you're new to your profession? Here are three things you can do: (1) Write down all the questions you're getting and position yourself as someone who is a learner, who is always taking time to develop professionally, and who has access to the information. (2) Schedule time every day to learn new content and never drop this habit. And (3) inform your prospects about your learning habits and goals and any classes or certifications in the works. This *is* powerful because everyone knows how rare this is regardless of age or experience.

IGNORANCE CAN BE BLISS

Interestingly, I have heard too many times for me to disbelieve that there are instances when some of your clients will respect you *more* when you tell them not to expect you to have all the answers. We can't pretend to know everything and certainly should not pretend to know something we don't.

Clearly this depends on your field to some extent. For example, I expect my dentist to know how to fix my teeth; I can't expect him to predict to the exact month how long his repair work on any one tooth will last (especially given my sweet tooth!).

A client of mine was telling me about some work she had done on her basement. While the initial work was done under contract, she had trusted her contractor enough to continue on with a second stage of work without putting anything formal in writing. It turns out that this contractor had never done this kind of work before but did not tell her.

Consequently, my client experienced an endless period of unmet deadlines, broken verbal commitments, and unreturned calls and e-mails because the contractor was trying to figure out how to do the work without admitting it. Needless to say, the frustration levels ran very high.

Even though the contractor was well liked by my client, this experience built up distrust. She recently told me that she could never recommend this contractor to anyone else.

KEEPING CURRENT

Here's what I recommend: develop the habit of reading something from your field at least three times per week for 30 minutes. First thing in the morning is usually the best time. It never ceases to amaze me how quickly I work in that new knowledge when talking with clients or presenting to groups. The ideas seem to sit there like freshly cooked meals waiting a few moments before being passed out by the wait staff at a busy restaurant and devoured by an appreciative audience.

I was traveling through Philadelphia recently and met a consultant named Joe Sharkey, who works all over the United States for a telecommunications company based in Utah. Thirty years ago Joe trained as an engineer, and so he knew all the technical aspects of his business. But it was only when he started helping the sales team of his company that he learned how to avoid technical jargon. "The bankers I meet with often tell me that I do a really good job explaining things in language they can understand."

Joe does such a good job explaining everything that now when he meets with investment bankers, his clients will invite peers so they can hear his expertise. His delivery is so compelling that they call him with referrals—although it did take him quite a few years to get to this point! So once you know your stuff, do your best to make sure that your clients truly understand everything you are saying.

In their book *Storyselling for Financial Advisors*, authors Scott West and Mitch Anthony argue that many clients walk away from meetings with advisors feeling confused because much of the language used was too technical. But the fear some salespeople have is that they are going to come across as unintelligent or average by speaking exclusively in layman's terms. Your clients do not want to feel foolish and may be wary of asking too many questions. Ask yourself if you might be using jargon as a crutch because you have not found a more effective way to communicate.

Exceed Your Customer and Employee Expectations by 1 Percent

Underpromise, overdeliver, and keep your word with clients and employees. You can't expect referrals if your service is simply what your client expects (average). That may sound totally obvious, but the next two points are not. In fact, there are two *big* problems with doing what you may well be doing now.

Satisfaction Is Average

I hear quite a lot from certain people about their customer satisfaction surveys and how well they have performed on them. Yet these people also get very few referrals. *Aiming simply for customer satisfaction is no longer adequate*—for retention or referrals!

In their book *Raving Fans*, Ken Blanchard and Sheldon Bowles state that satisfied customers are satisfied *sheep* "just parked on your doorstep until something better comes along." You have to do more than that to keep your clients as repeat business and have them endorse you to others.

Sales guru Jeffrey Gitomer makes an amusing point about what's most important: would you rather have your spouse be loyal, or would you settle for your spouse just being satisfied?

Customer Service Is Not Enough

Almost all businesspeople think their customer service is what sets them apart! Please stop and think about this for a moment. How many times have you heard another professional say that what makes his or her business better than the competition is customer service? This can't be. So be brutally honest with yourself and ask, "Is what I do really any different or better? How is it truly better?" I suspect that often we tell ourselves that simply because *we* show up, it has to be better. That's like saying the Audubon Society should put each of us on the endangered species list because there's only one of us!

Aiming for wow customer service is a worthy goal to pursue from time to time, but it is not a sustainable business practice. If someone comes into an insurance agent's office to make a monthly car insurance payment, is it fair to expect the agent to send flowers or mail a gift certificate for a steakhouse? That would be absurd.

Many of our frustrations with people who get our business is that they don't even do what they say they're going to do. As basic as it sounds, start by keeping your word. I know I've made the mistake of casually saying, "Sure, I'll get that out to you tomorrow," without bothering to remember that I will be traveling all day tomorrow! It does work much better to suggest that you will have the information somewhat later than even you expect so you exceed their expectations.

HOW CAN I IMPROVE THE SERVICE MY CLIENTS GET?

Three years ago I did a workshop in Massachusetts for a financial advisor and his referral group, which consisted of influential professionals in his community. When I saw his office, he had it all: an electronic sign with the names of clients coming in that day; classical music playing in the background; china cups and quality coffee, muffins, and cookies in a basket; unique artwork and interesting framed pictures; sports memorabilia signed by well-known coaches and athletes from the Red Sox, Celtics, and Patriots; a broad choice of current magazines; and an elaborate aquarium. He also had a high-end follow-up system that he implemented once a client had visited. There is likely more that I have forgotten. It was remarkable; it made me feel classy and appreciated. And anyone can start this process. He had been in business for 25 years, and he had instituted many ideas he'd learned from conferences over the years.

Despite the wealth of knowledge available today about best business practices, isn't it bizarre that most of us have *low* expectations as customers, that most of the time we expect to be underwhelmed and to deal with people who care little? It is why I believe there is great reason to be optimistic about the future of personal service businesses: We all need quality people we can depend on. We all seek that go-to resource in various areas in a world of rapid change and many fleeting virtual relationships. That businessperson might as well be you. The competition is not all that stiff!

DON'T FORGET ABOUT YOUR EMPLOYEES!

According to Gallup's Peter Flade, having emotionally engaged employees is as important as having happy customers. How come nobody seems to talk about this?

Sam Walton learned this lesson 30 years ago. His employees had a poor reputation for how well they were treating customers. What he learned was that if his managers treated his employees well, the happy employees would then be nicer to the customers, who would then have a positive shopping experience. In the book *Business Leaders and Success*, Walton noted "the customers will return again and again, and that is where the real profit in this business lies." It was an innovative way to gauge customer satisfaction that proved very effective. And it all started at the top.

Advantages also include employees who are more productive, stay with your company longer, are absent less, and have a better safety record. All of which also means lower training and replacement expenses for you.

Sean, one of the sales managers I currently coach to get referrals for recruiting prospects, has started taking one of his reps out for lunch each week. It has been a huge success. He asks them to block out two hours. The bulk of the meeting (and the primary goal) is focused on how they are doing and how he can help them improve in their business.

He takes on the role of coach, offering specific positive feedback, support, accountability, and direction on what they are not seeing about their performance. The atmosphere is more relaxed and conducive to more open dialogue, which means making an emotional connection away from the hustle of the office, the multiple phone calls, and sales appointments. It's a distraction-free environment (unless the wait staff is cute!) where it is easier to show that he truly cares.

And there is a win for Sean. His reps are expected to come with three referrals for him (he aims high, and they average one quality referral each time). The win for the reps is that they can take on a leadership role in helping the person they recommend succeed because they know they are bringing that person onto a winning team. Sean has created his own additional rewards as well after asking his reps what else would motivate them.

Strong customer (and employee) service is a must in order to earn the right to ask for referrals and to expect them.

CHAPTER 3

BECOMING FEARLESS

The brave man is not he who does not feel afraid but he who conquers fear.

—Nelson Mandela

The vast majority of people I coach and meet have reservations about asking for all they want. Frankly, almost everyone feels bashful much of the time. I would like to share the lessons they have learned so that you can get the results you want far sooner.

FACE YOUR FEAR OF REJECTION AND FEAR OF PEOPLE

While most of us hate to admit it, let's come clean about our primary challenge. Most people in sales are, at best, uncomfortable contacting strangers and uncomfortable meeting them. At worst, they can't even pick up the phone because they're fearful of the responses they might get and afraid that their feelings might get hurt.

The same is often true when asking for referrals. The vast majority of people are not comfortable doing it, and I see lack of comfort as the main obstacle for most people.

You don't need a Ph.D. in psychology to know that the solution is to face your fears. It's not easy. If it were easy, everyone would make many more sales and the turnover in your industry would be much, much lower.

What matters is that you develop the mindset that people want what you have to offer. Your belief that you truly can make a difference makes all the difference! It's called congruent communication.

STOP HESITATING AND START SUCCEEDING

In his audio program *The Psychology of Sales*, Brian Tracy gives the perfect example when he suggests that you imagine that you have been given a long list of people who all want to buy what you sell, but you only have until midnight to contact them. He asks, "What time would you start that day? How late would you work? Would you find other things to do before making your calls? Would you take coffee breaks? Would you take an hour for lunch? No! You would be contacting as many people as possible! There would be no hesitation!"

When facing your fears, the reminders you need as often as necessary are that:

1. **You admit to yourself the truth and not blame other things.** Don't lay blame, for example, on not having a polished referral script, elevator speech, or high-end sales materials to hand out.

2. **You get enough leverage on yourself to face your fears.** This is based on what I covered in Chapter 1: you act when either the pain gets too great (dissatisfaction can be a good driver) or the pleasure juices you up enough to be driven to take more action. That's your responsibility.

3. **You know that most people are also afraid of you and worry that you will judge and reject them!** It's time to start noticing

that most people avoid your eye contact in public and avoid inter-acting with you. Frankly, it is unbelievable! Be more aware of this fear that others have and make a mental shift—use this knowledge to empower yourself. Say to yourself, "They might be uncomfort-able too; I should put their mind at ease. I am not a shark. If they're interested, great, I can help them. And if they're not inter-ested, it's okay—not everyone is going to be interested."

4. **You focus on helping the other person.** The founder of Mary Kay Cosmetics had a great saying that everyone has an invis-ible sign around the neck that says "Make me feel important." Yes, it's an intelligent way to treat someone, and, yes, it also reduces a person's fears; but most important, it gets your focus off yourself and onto something constructive. Your fears will be reduced.

5. **You remember that how you look at any situation in life is a choice!** Every way you interpret a situation can be looked at in a completely different way. There are people who go through a relationship breakup and are empowered to finally be free of something negative; other people are devastated and vow never to be hurt so much again (it took me more years than I care to remember to realize I had done that one to myself). There are salespeople out there who truly enjoy doing the things that make others uncomfortable. As Stephen Covey says, "If you want to change your life, you've got to change your paradigms."

FACE IT SOME MORE!

What's the number one need almost every business owner and sales-person has? More prospects, right?

Fear of rejection is very often the main obstacle to contacting and meeting more prospects. The solution is to face your fears more and more by building your "courage muscle." I know from my own experience that this is much easier said than done.

I truly hope that the following three incredible stories help you face your fears better and see them in a truer perspective.

RAOUL WALLENBERG

This Swedish banker had a very comfortable life in a neutral country during World War II. Even though he wasn't Jewish himself, he was so outraged by what the Nazis were doing, that he chose to go to Hungary, one of the world's most chaotic and unsafe places in July 1944, to save as many Jews as he could from extermination. His accomplishments are remarkable.

Want courage? When Jews were being rounded up to be taken to the death camps, he would calmly walk up to the SS commander and tell him that he had Swedish protection passes and that if any Jews were taken away, this commander would be reported and hanged as a war criminal. He saved as many as 25,000 Jews this way even though he forged many of the passes. As many as 25,000! One eyewitness recalled:

> *He stood out there in the street, probably feeling [like] the loneliest man in the world, trying to pretend that there was something behind him. They could have shot him there and then in the street and nobody would have known about it.*

On another occasion, he actually invited Adolf Eichmann, head of operations for Hitler's Final Solution, over for dinner. Eichmann was obsessed with wiping Jews out of existence. Yet Wallenberg told him that the Nazis were going to lose the war, and then he explained why Nazi ideology was so flawed. Eichmann was so enraged by this that he told Wallenberg, "Accidents do happen, even to a neutral diplomat."

Wallenberg disappeared once the Soviets arrived and is believed to have died at age 33 in one of their gulag camps.

Would you have the courage to do this knowing you would likely never see your home country and family again? Is it really so uncomfortable to ask for that referral when you've helped someone out?

MARTIN LUTHER KING JR.

Picture this: It's January 1956. Your newborn is asleep in her cot, and your young spouse is fast asleep too. But your house was recently firebombed, and you've had numerous death threats. It's after midnight, and you're sitting alone at the kitchen table with a cold cup of coffee. You've just received another phone call telling you to get out of town before you or your wife and child will be killed. What would you do?

It was at this point that Martin Luther King Jr., found that his courage had deserted him. He was terrified and had a panicked conversation with God. "I tried to think of a way to move out of the picture without appearing a coward. I got to the point that I couldn't take it any longer. I was weak."

Was a seat on a city bus worth putting his family at risk?

As he prayed, he "could hear the quiet assurance of an inner voice saying, 'Martin Luther, stand up for righteousness. Stand up for justice. Stand up for truth.' At that moment I experienced the presence of the Divine as I had never experienced Him before. Almost at once my fears began to go."

Over the years, the death threats continued, and King was assassinated 12 years later in 1968 at age 39.

I understand that the cause of our livelihood is likely not as momentous as King's. But if King faced death threats for over a decade, how long do you think it would take for you to get past your prospecting fears if you faced them every day with the same amount of courage? Everyone concurs that our fear diminishes when we confront it over and over.

Aung San Suu Kyi

She was the world's most renowned female prisoner of conscience for almost 20 years until 2010. While living a very comfortable life in England as a wife of an Oxford professor and a mother, she returned to her home country, Burma, in 1988 as prodemocracy movements swept the country.

Her father had secured independence for Burma from the British in 1947, but he was assassinated that same year. So she decided to fulfill her duty to a father and country she loved.

Despite preaching nonviolent protest and despite being democratically elected in 1990 to be prime minister (with 81 percent of the votes!), she was under house arrest without charge from July 1989 to November 2010—more than 20 years! Courage? Her arrest came on a day when she and some of her colleagues confronted the soldiers in an army unit, who were pointing their guns at her. Rather than surrender, she walked toward them alone, offering herself as an easy target.

Her best-known writings are called *Freedom from Fear*; can you apply this to your business?

> *Fearlessness may be a gift, but perhaps more precious is the courage acquired through endeavor; courage that comes from cultivating the habit of refusing to let fear dictate one's actions, courage that could be described as "grace under pressure"— grace which is renewed repeatedly in the face of harsh, unremitting pressure.*

Aung San Suu Kyi won the Nobel Peace Prize in 1991. In May 2008, when Cyclone Nargis hit Burma, Suu Kyi lost her roof and was living in virtual darkness after she lost electricity in her dilapi-dated lakeside bungalow. She is now 66 years old and has rarely been allowed to see her two children since 1988. She always had the option to leave Burma and live in comfort, but she refused since she would never be allowed to return and fight for democracy.

Got the courage to sustain your beliefs about what's right for 20 years despite being confined to your decaying house by a paranoid military dictatorship? How long have you been uncomfortable about asking for referrals? Do you have it in you to push through this? How long might that take?

Courage

Three people who could all have chosen a quiet, comfortable life and never have made an impact. They all learned how to find more cour-age. You are not being asked to put your life on the line or your family's safety at stake. What do you want out of your life? Is it time to hold your chin up higher and say, "I'm not walking into a life-threatening situation. I am extending my help to others. I believe in what I'm doing. If they don't want it, that's their loss. I will move on and show more courage. If it was easy, everyone would do it. I intend to do it."

As humans we are all made of the same stuff. What are you made of, and how much of this is showing?

Overcome the Biggest Myth in Our Culture

Some time ago, I was invited to the annual awards banquet of an inter-national financial services company. When the top producer for the year walked up to the podium to "say a few words," I was not expect-ing to hear anything earth-shattering. What he said was amazing and inspiring. First he told his life story with such passion that it took my breath away. He was a former teacher (like me) who now absolutely loved what he did. He was living his mission, not working a job.

Then he asked those in the audience who were in their first five years in the industry to stand up. I expected the speaker would offer a motivational plug to them, but instead he looked them in the eye and explained how they would never know how many times he had felt like a failure. He shared that he almost quit on numerous occasions in his early years and that he even kept his teaching license current just in case. Most highly accomplished people have fallen on their faces many times, but they keep getting up.

The myth in our culture is that it's mostly naturals who make it big with little effort.

Here are three priceless observations on "failure":

♦ Relationship expert Barbara DeAngelis points out that "the only path to success is to do it badly first."

♦ Billionaire rebel Richard Branson once said of his accomplishments, "I've just failed a lot more than most people."

♦ *Success Intelligence* author Robert Holden states that most people define successful people as "people who have not failed at anything."

Clearly, it's a huge myth in our culture that high-achieving people were all overnight sensations, that getting to the top was a pretty seamless experience for them, and that their success is the result of innate talent.

DEMYSTIFYING THE MYTH

Contrary, there have been many well-known people who have had all kinds of rejections and failures but have become successful "because they have used their failures well." Here are a few classic examples from Holden's book:

As a composer, he is hopeless.
> —A music teacher referring to one of his students,
> Ludwig van Beethoven

He has no talent at all, that boy ... Tell him please to give up painting.
> —Edouard Manet to Claude Monet, 1864,
> about Renoir

He is too stupid to learn anything and should think of a career where he might succeed by virtue of his pleasant personality.
> —A teacher writing about his student
> Thomas Edison

Can't act. Can't sing. Balding. Can dance a little.
> —MGM executive commenting on a screen test by an
> aspiring entertainer called Fred Astaire, 1928

He lacked imagination and had no good ideas.
> —Newspaper editor after firing his employee,
> Walt Disney

You'd better learn secretarial work or else get married.
> —Director of Blue Book Modeling Agency to would-be
> actress Marilyn Monroe, 1944

You ought to go back to drivin' a truck.
> —The theater manager who fired a singer called
> Elvis Presley after one performance, 1954

We don't think your ideas have any merit here.

> —IBM executive to a young man named Bill Gates

You'll never make any money out of children's books.

> —The publisher who took on J. K. Rowling's first Harry Potter book (Rowling is now the highest-earning woman in England at $1 billion.)

Following Failure with Success

So what can you do to achieve your dream of being a high achiever?

1. **Realize that falling on your face is normal.** Have you ever come across a biography of anyone who reached a significant goal who did not face adversity? Excuse my cliché, but we all have to stumble around before we crawl, crawl before we can walk, and walk before we can run. Getting good at generating referrals is no different.

2. **Develop a support system.** The high achiever who spoke at the financial services company awards banquet I wrote about earlier said he could not have done what he's done without the unconditional support of his spouse. He went on further to say that without a supportive spouse you could not fulfill your potential.

   What is your support system? You can get creative about this (beyond people). It can include anything empowering that makes you feel good: audio programs, books, photos, inspiring music and literature, pets, or even locations. Build a support team around you (see Chapter 7 for more on this). I believe it also means minimizing time with energy vampires—negative people. You become the sum of the people you spend the most time with.

3. **Build empowering beliefs about yourself.** You can only expect others to open doors for you when you have enough faith in yourself that you are the right person for the job. For more on this, see the section "Become Your Number One Fan" in Chapter 4.

4. **Define success and failure for yourself.** You decide your own definition of success. For example, "I did my best and learned something." You decide when you deserve to feel like a failure. This might be when you have not kept your word or perhaps haven't lived according to your values. This is infinitely superior to feeling bad because your house isn't as large as someone else's or because someone makes more money than you.

The ultimate belief is to accept that failure is only a necessary and normal part of the journey.

STOP MAKING EXCUSES

How much responsibility do you really take—for your life and your referral business?

On a scale of 1 to 10, how much responsibility do you take for everything in your life? I think this is an area where we fool ourselves.

WHO IS RESPONSIBLE?

Who do you suppose said this? "I have spent the best years of my life giving people the lighter pleasures—helping them have a good time. And all I get is abuse: the existence of a hunted man."

It was Al Capone. I spent an entire semester of college in 1989 doing a U.S. history independent study on Capone and organized crime in Chicago in the 1920s. Without going into detail, he either personally killed or sentenced dozens of people to premature and violent death.

A recent newspaper headline story was about a 23-year-old woman who had killed her youngest child. Her reason? "I only have enough love for one child."

Thinking about these examples, I can't help but recall all the feeble excuses I heard from students about not doing homework when I was teaching. "Who's responsible for doing your work?" I would ask, and there would usually be an awkward silence followed by a quiet "I am." Did it make a difference? I failed more students than any other teacher—but those who passed only did so because they took my lesson to heart. If grade school students can learn responsibility for their actions, so can professional adults.

THE RESPONSIBILITY SCALE

Several years ago I went to a Brian Tracy seminar. During the first break I went up to talk to him. I guess I really didn't think through what I wanted to ask him. I just wanted to talk to him in person. He had been telling his remarkable life story for 90 minutes and weaving in what it took to be successful. All I could muster was a vague "Your story is amazing. How did you do it?" He looked slightly exasperated as if to say, "Weren't you listening to anything I just said?"

Then he thought for a moment and told me about how he had been so poor in his early twenties that he would save money on cooking by heating his can of beans on the radiator overnight. *Then one day as he looked around his bleak living space, he realized that he had no one else to blame but himself.* It was no longer legitimate to blame parents or teachers. Everything he had in life was up to him.

Then he said to me, "If I had to just pinpoint one thing, I think we all have a responsibility scale inside us. And most people are probably at about a 6. And what I've learned is that you have to move yourself to a 10, take complete ownership of every area of your life, and refuse to blame anyone or anything else."

Who's responsible for your results? Your health? Your relationships? Your inner peace? Your income?

If you don't like the results you're getting, look at your actions. In many respects, this is a tough pill to swallow for most people, but it's also very exciting and very empowering.

HOW MUCH RESPONSIBILITY DO YOU TAKE FOR YOUR REFERRAL BUSINESS?

Think about these questions as you assess your position on the responsibility scale. To score a 10 on this means you are answering yes to each of the questions and taking complete ownership of your results:

1. **Do you always ask for your referrals?** "Forgetting to ask" is excuse number one that people have for not asking. It is too convenient to "forget a lot" rather than to admit being uncomfortable and fearful. You have to take responsibility for the things you do that get in your own way, for your limiting beliefs, and for your courage.

   Do a mini interview with others. Ask them what they think your strengths are, and ask them how they think you're getting in your own way.

2. **Do you follow your own agenda?** Start using meeting agendas and putting something nonthreatening on them like "feedback" instead of "introductions," from which you can pivot to other people that your client would like to help by recommending you. (For more on agendas, see Chapter 5.)

3. **Do you ever take "I can't think of anyone" for an answer?** Everybody knows 200 people or more. Provided your client talks about the value you have brought (and actually gets specific—not

just a nod of the head), it is *your* job to help your client think of someone. Most people like to help others. Ask better questions that help jog their memories. Show more confidence in yourself and bring home the point that you can help people your clients care about. Never accept it when someone suggests you contact others but do not use their name. Find out why or pursue a better referral. (For more on this, see Chapter 6.)

4. **Do you have a script?** If you have no concerns about asking, have you developed wording that works for you?

5. **Do you plant the seeds about referrals with an expectations discussion?** When you first meet prospects, this is your chance to explain how much they can expect from you. And it's a chance for you to explain what you want from a client relationship in return. Assuming you have done a good job, it should not be unreasonable to request that clients consider endorsing you to others that they care about because you could probably help them too. (See Chapter 5 for more on this topic.)

6. **Do you narrow down referral requests?** How well do you identify specific referral requests? Can you word your request so that two to three people automatically come to mind when you ask? (See Chapter 6.)

7. **Do you educate your clients?** Have you developed materials or wording to educate your clients on what a quality referral for you would be? (See Chapter 6.)

8. **Do you reassure your clients?** How well do you reassure your clients about how you follow up and how you don't expect them to know for sure whether the people they recommend have a need for what you do? (See Chapter 6.)

9. **Do you coach your clients?** Do you coach your clients on what to say to the people they recommend—most of them have no idea what to say! It's your job to do this. (See Chapter 6.)

10. **Do you keep control of the referral process?** Do you make sure you always have the next step in the referral process so that you can keep control? (See Chapter 6.)

11. **Do you have a great follow-up system ... and use it?** Do you have a follow-up system in place so you don't drop the ball on names you do receive and have a means to thank your referral sources? (See Chapter 7.)

12. **Have you developed and utilized centers of influence?** Have you developed four to five great centers of influence as referral sources? Centers of influence are simply people who can open bigger and better doors for you. Some may be clients, other professionals, or even people in your own family.

    Centers of influence are a topic worthy of their own book (one I may in fact write one day). My first suggestion to you is to focus on your strongest relationships that fit the above definition, keep pouring water in those wells, and use steps 3, 5, and 6 from the Six-Step Fearless Referral Conversation to make it easy for centers of influence to help you.

13. **Do you plan ahead?** Do you plan your weeks ahead of time to proactively schedule time to do these things? (See Chapter 7.)

14. **Are you your own role model?** Since there may not be anyone in your office who can serve as a great role model, take 100 percent responsibility for your referral business. If you're not happy with it, only you can do something about it. No quick-fix leads program is going to transform your financial situation.

See what I mean? Getting to a 10 on the responsibility scale is not easy! We don't like to admit we've made a mistake, done something wrong, or not taken complete responsibility. What we blame is in our self-talk and the excuses we give to others. The hope is that this will increase your own self-awareness and help you move toward that 10.

Use this book as your solution to getting referrals your way and developing your own personal system. *You are responsible for developing a system that works for you because there is no one-size-fits-all when it comes to getting referrals.*

GET COMFORTABLE GETTING UNCOMFORTABLE

Asking for referrals makes many salespeople feel uncomfortable. While this book has as many suggestions and solutions as can be imagined to get past that, the reality may well still be that you have to face some fear if you are going to succeed! There is no quick-fix alternative.

The only question is, how much do you want what you say you want? How motivated are you? Usually, getting out of our comfort zone means changing. Why don't we like to change?

We get used to doing things a certain way and often resent interruptions to our "comfortable" status quo.

We get hardwired to act, think, and behave a specific—automated—way, in many instances without even realizing our reactions are not thought through.

Then, even worse, we say, "This is just the way I am!"

This is an enormously important point. When we grow up, we get used to thinking and feeling a certain way in different situations. Regardless of whether this is positive or negative, it becomes our norm. *Because it is our norm—because we've gotten used to it—it also becomes comfortable—even when it is negative or ho-hum.* You might want to read that again.

Negative or mediocre mindsets can be comfortable for some people. I was astonished when I realized this was true for me one weekend when I was making no serious attempt to get out of an uninspired mood. I realized that in my dim and distant past, feeling that way was something I was used to. I was alarmed because I had fooled myself into thinking I was completely past that. I had also fooled myself into believing that it was comfortable and therefore a good thing. Only the dull pain of a nagging negativity clued me into the realization of how unmotivated I was feeling.

When it comes to pursuing more referrals, it is vital therefore to understand that even though we are used to our feelings and our comfort zone, the likelihood is that it is not helping us grow our business and meet all the people we need to meet.

Doing something new can create anxiety and a crisis in confidence.

The best suggestion I can make is that you step out of your comfort zone a few small steps at a time. Remember, growth only happens outside your comfort zone.

Even though change is a fact of life, many of us resist it and are frustrated every time it happens. Yet (as I'm sure you've heard many times!), if you keep doing what you've been doing, you'll keep getting what you've always gotten.

So first recognize what you are doing now that you (1) want to stop doing, (2) want to do less, (3) want to continue doing, (4) want to do more, and (5) want to start doing. By the time you've finished this book, you should have several things to add to item 3 and also be ready to spend less time on some other things that are comfortable but not getting you the referrals you want!

Second, once you recognize what you're doing now, ask yourself what's comfortable. Most of the time our habits and moods are a comfort zone for us, and we do not realize it. Think back to how alive (and, yes, how scared) you felt when you first started in business. Nothing was comfortable, right? Then you let that muscle get flabby and untested. This all relates to self-awareness.

Third, moving past this discomfort (starting a new habit) takes a great deal of effort early on. It's a bit like the needs of a rocket. Most of the energy it uses is required at takeoff, and once it has taken off, it needs very little to do all the other remarkable things it needs to do. Similarly, as you launch some new habits that feel awkward, most of your effort will come at the start.

Ron was a client of mine for some time, and we were spinning our wheels until I told him that if he wanted to succeed in his business, he was going to have to face his fear of prospecting and people saying no. Once he decided to face this almost every day, he started to make great strides, setting up more appointments, coffees—asking for what he wanted! He changed his mindset into seeing prospecting as a new challenge that could be fun, almost a game. It wasn't so easy that he felt this way all day long, but his new empowering mindset got him taking constructive action more and more consistently.

There are no secrets to success!

Identify Your Obstacles about Asking for Referrals

Why don't we take action after coming across a great idea?

About four years ago I went to a Wealth Expo in Chicago featuring Donald Trump and Robert Kiyosaki and was fortunate enough to see Tony Robbins there. He had 9,000 people jumping up and down, cheering loudly, and running up and hugging total strangers. I—yes, Mr. Reserved Englishman—was one of them. It sounds really far-fetched, but I know that some of you reading this have had the same experience somewhere.

He pointed out that most people would do nothing with his "life-changing" information. He told everyone to take notes so they would remember what he had talked about. I looked around closely; maybe 1 in 20 attendees heeded his advice. Let me be clear: I was impressed that day. He hit on numerous vital issues.

But the other remarkable part was how quickly the energy level changed the minute it was over. As I walked out in this flood of 9,000, I could hear conversations on either side of me. Nobody was talking about what they were going to do next to improve their lives. All I could hear were people saying, "Yes it was good, but," and finding a flaw in one of Robbins's points, identifying reasons why his seminar had not "worked" for them. Once I left that auditorium, the atmosphere could not have been more different. There was nothing positive or inspiring about it: it was a feeding frenzy of get-rich-quick schemes and sales sharks.

So why is it that 98 percent of people do nothing after hearing a great idea—including after reading a book?

Obstacles

Why aren't most people getting the referrals they want? I think there are four primary reasons:

1. **Outdated ideas.** The current concerns you have right now about asking for referrals get in your way; you need to see these from now on as simply old beliefs that aren't true anymore. *This is arguably the most important point I make in this entire book!*

2. **Lack of belief.** You have to believe that you are capable of doing it and that generating referrals is a skill you can develop (see Chapter 1).

3. **Low expectations.** You have to believe (more and more) that you deserve referrals and expect them. If you don't really believe this, you will become a self-fulfilling prophecy and not succeed. To change your beliefs, see Chapter 4.

4. **Low self-image.** Who you think you can become is the best indicator of who you will become. Where you see yourself in

the future is crucial if you want to trend upward on whatever achievement scale that matters to you. If you don't think much of yourself, you're stacking the deck against the likelihood of success. One powerful solution to this is to start visualizing yourself having the lifestyle you want (more on this in Chapter 4).

Asking for what you want sounds so simple. Yet it is a real challenge for many because—unless finding the right wording is your only challenge—you have to confront your fear. Why are we afraid to ask? Often it is:

1. Fear of looking pushy
2. Fear of looking needy
3. Fear of looking foolish
4. Fear of being rejected and hearing no

In Chapter 1, I wrote about the fixed versus the growth mindset, asking for a referral and fearing that it might not go that well. In other words, making a mistake—experiencing failure—is going to be very hard for you if you have more of a fixed mindset and believe that your ability is mostly fixed.

When it comes to asking for referrals, other common concerns are:

1. Fear of sounding cheesy or canned
2. Fear of spoiling a good relationship
3. Uncertainty about when to ask
4. Uncertainty about what to say

Do any of these resonate for you? Being aware of why you are fearful or apprehensive is a mandatory place to start—provided you don't give it unnecessary validation. If you argue for your weakness, it's yours.

While these are the most frequently mentioned, there are plenty of other irrational things some people tell themselves.

Sometimes people need to talk for a few minutes about referral-asking concerns before their own concern "pops" and they happen to mention something. Here are some things I've heard in the past:

◆ "Well, for people to refer me, they need to have seen the work that I do for at least a couple of years."

◆ "If I get paid by doing business with them, I feel like I've been compensated and shouldn't be asking for more."

◆ "I don't want my clients to feel like they're part-time salespeople for me."

◆ "I don't like making my clients feel uncomfortable" (even though it is *you* who is really the uncomfortable one making others feel the same way).

Yet others have other concerns such as:

◆ "I don't want to lose the sale by asking them for something else."

◆ "I don't know how to retreat if the person is unwilling to suggest anyone."

And the most dangerous and unempowering: "If I just give great customer service, the referrals should come without me having to ask."

SOLUTIONS

What are some ways to get over these fears so you can get more referrals?

Identify Concerns

First, you've got to identify the unhelpful concerns you have about asking. Make sure you have a clear understanding about why you don't ask. Take a few minutes and answer this question, "What concerns do I have about asking for referrals?"

DO IT!

Grab a sheet of paper and list the numbers 1 to 3. Next to each number write down a concern you've expressed or thought about in regard to asking for referrals. If you can think of more, add them! The point is to get your concerns out into the open so you can finally deal with them and then move on.

Understanding this is crucial! Do not skip this part—we'll come back to it later in the book. Be completely honest with yourself. You will make no progress without being clear about what the enemy looks like.

Understand That Your "Concerns" Are Beliefs

Beliefs are powerful. Unhelpful ones must be changed for you to get positive results. Changing beliefs can be a meaty topic, and for *most* people this is not a simple undertaking. Yet if these unhelpful beliefs are not changed, you will not make progress.

Know That Your Beliefs Determine All Results in Every Area of Your Life

Your beliefs influence everything. They drive your feelings, they sway your actions, and they preview your results.

If your belief is "I think it's pushy to ask," then when you have a meeting, what are your feelings? With a belief like that, at the moment of opportunity you'll most likely look inside and decide "I feel very uncomfortable asking for referrals today."

If your belief that asking is "pushy" yields a feeling of discomfort, what action do you think you will follow?

You probably won't ask.

What results do you get? Nothing positive. You generate no new business opportunity, and you have not reached out and offered to help others.

If you believe "Why on earth wouldn't people want to recommend me?" your feelings are confident.

Feeling confident, you will ask for referrals if the meeting goes well; and if you keep asking, you'll get results.

We will build on the relationship between beliefs and results in Chapter 6, and if you follow the steps detailed there (and believe in the process), you will get more and more referrals.

FOLLOW YOUR OWN EXAMPLE

Ask yourself, why do you refer other professionals to people you care about? That will reveal the qualities that really matter to you. When I do this with groups, the list is consistently short: honest, nice, competent, integrity and trust, punctual, good service, fair price, respectful, follows up promptly. Sometimes people add likeable, experienced, and sense of humor.

Now that you've asked yourself to identify the qualities you value and you've got them fresh in your mind (or even better, jotted down in the margins), look in the mirror. Do you fit that bill?

How do you match up? Look at that list like you're looking in the mirror. If you feel confident that you are all these things, that's great.

What this really means is facing the truth: You are good enough. You do deserve to get referrals from others.

Be a Better Resource to Others

If you don't refer much business to others, it's time to change. I find there is a direct correlation between the amount of business we refer and the amount we receive. I admit that adding value to others is what matters most; referrals can play a key part in this. If you are untrusting by nature, I believe you subconsciously send the same message when *asking* for referrals. Reread the Rule of Reciprocation!

So how do you change your beliefs? Funny you should ask. Turn to Chapter 4 and let's get started.

Fearless Referral Asking

*If you believe in your value, how could it possibly be
appropriate to hide it from people who need it?*

—T. Harv Eker

Become Your Number One Fan

You need to truly believe in what you bring to the table. Why? So you know you deserve and therefore should expect referrals. There should be nothing more to think about unless the person you're asking is negatively disrupted by something in his life or has an adverse relationship with the person you want him to talk to.

Create empowering beliefs about asking based on the value you bring. Here are some beliefs that can empower you to ask for referrals:

1. I am as good as anyone else who does what I do.

2. My company is one of the best.

3. I truly care about helping people.

4. My clients are truly better off because of doing business with me.

5. My clients should benefit by recommending me because I am going to make them look good and get them positive feedback from those they refer!

You have to feel very good about what you do (and who you are) and understand that giving others the chance to recommend people they care about to you is the biggest no-brainer in the world.

The first thing I expect new clients of mine to do is make a list of reasons that others would factor when choosing to do business with them. It may seem like too elementary of an exercise, but all communication starts with you. You have to be your number one fan and be confident in the difference you make. This is one way to get crystal clear about it. If you were going to list reasons why you should marry someone and could only come up with three, you'd be wise to reconsider!

Now, take some time to complete the list discussed below. Think hard about this list. Often the most impactful ideas are the ones later in the list. Skip this exercise at your peril!

DO IT!

List all the value you bring to the table. Make this a list of 20 qualities that describe you and how you do business, perhaps things happy clients have said. Then add more to it. This essentially states, "I believe I'm really good at what I do, and here's why." The more you reinforce this confidence, the better, because you will find it easier to ask for referrals.

20 Reasons Why People Should Do Business with Me

1. _____   6. _____

2. _____   7. _____

3. _____   8. _____

4. _____   9. _____

5. _____   10. _____

11. _____   16. _____

12. _____   17. _____

13. _____   18. _____

14. _____   19. _____

15. _____   20. _____

Once you've completed your list, circle the top five reasons that resonate most loudly with you and keep them top of mind by posting them somewhere—perhaps by your computer or on your bathroom mirror. Revisit this list regularly and keep adding to it. The goal here is for you to recognize all you do bring to the table so that you communicate in a compelling way. Remember, sales is a transfer of enthusiasm!

Last year I did a Webcast for a large company with one of the company's advisors, Eric. Eric has been very good at getting referrals over the years. When we were rehearsing for the event, I asked him what he said to himself (i.e., what his belief is) when it came to asking others for referrals.

Weirdly, he couldn't think of an answer. Ten minutes later, as we were talking about something else, he interrupted the conversation and said, "Matt! *'Why on earth would you not be working with me?'*— that's what I say to myself; that's my attitude." Only some time later did I realize that the reason it took Eric so long to think of this was that it's hardwired for him now so he's less conscious of it—it's second nature and now on autopilot. But once upon a time, landing on that belief gave him the confidence to ask more.

A current client of mine, Corey, used to physically squirm at the prospect of asking for referrals. After doing his 20 reasons, he saw that he was very good at what he did and that it really made no sense that he wasn't asking more. He said to me, "Matt, *if not me—then who?* Why shouldn't I be the one to ask for their business? I'm as good as anyone is at this—and, frankly, I think I'm better."

Here's the most important part: he did not transform overnight into an asking machine (some people do, but most need more repetition). Almost every day after our session he would repeat, "If not me, then who?" In fact, almost every time I talked to him, he would repeat the statement. For two or three months I thought nothing of it. Then as his results continued to get better, I remembered how often he said that. I asked him whether he thought he had been rewiring his brain with a new belief these past months, or was I just trying to be an amateur psychologist? He wholeheartedly agreed that he now had a new belief about asking. *Because he has consistently repeated this new belief, he has made huge changes in the number of referrals he gets—and he asks for more business in other areas too.*

As soon as you have the conviction to look your clients in the eye and say, "I know I can help many of the people you care about," you're set (even if the words you use are softer).

HELP VERSUS SELL

I met Melissa at a top producer panel at her company's national sales congress before I was due to speak. We were talking about fear of rejection and approaching people for business. First I asked her what she said when she called people. She explained that she had no script or magic words; she just really believed that people should meet her. I concluded that her confident tone was what made the difference—her conviction she was worth meeting.

But I was concerned that the other producers in her audience that day watching the panel discussion would dismiss her courage as a quality they did not have and therefore dismiss her ideas.

So I asked her where she got her thick skin such that she was not afraid to call people.

"That's easy. When I was 21 I got a job selling cars, and I had to deal with a *lot* of rejection. But that's not what makes the calling easy. When I sold cars, there were times when I sold people cars that they didn't really need and couldn't always afford. As a financial advisor, I am not trying to sell them anything. My job is to help people. Picking up the phone is easy."

The moral here is to believe more and more that you are helping, not trying to sell. The more you believe this, the easier the asking will be. I've retold Melissa's story to countless clients to help them smash the belief that asking for a referral is the same as trying to "sell" their clients one more thing. One client of mine, Penny, needed to hear Melissa's story to move on from her outdated and inaccurate ideas concerning referrals. Even after being in my coaching program for a few months she was still feeling bashful when it mattered most. I told her, "You're not selling; you're helping—helping yourself and your business and also helping your referral sources and clients help others."

THE REFERRAL MINDSET YOU MUST HAVE

What's the Referral Mindset? It's, *"I'm good at what I do. I can help people you care about. And I know I probably need to ask you."* That's it. Once you adopt this, asking for referrals continues to get easier until it's a completely obvious thing for you to do.

DO IT!

Put the Referral Mindset on a Post-it note or an index card and put it somewhere highly visible.

Another tremendously useful exercise to help you change any unhelpful belief is to first identify what empowering belief you need; for example, "People like to help me" or "People like to refer me."

Then, *start a list of evidence that proves this belief to be true.* Write down all the people over the years who have tried to open doors for you (even if it didn't lead to business) in different ways. Add those people who have given you ideas and information that have helped your business and professional development and start the process of rewiring your brain away from your unhelpful beliefs. Prove to your brain that your new belief is true and keep that list visible until your brain has fully bought into it.

DO IT!

Write out a list of people who have tried to open doors for you. Look at this list and know that their actions prove their belief in you. If they believe in you, you should believe in yourself.

Three final reminders on changing your unhelpful beliefs about asking for referrals:

1. Focus on the reasons why you should ask for referrals.

2. Work consistently on building yourself up. This is the part of your conscious and subconscious thinking that you want to grow—not the unhelpful beliefs that have led to the underwhelming results so far! You can't expect other people to be enthusiastic about recommending you if they sense you are unsure of yourself.

3. Take time during the day to acknowledge yourself for all the little things you did right. Some days I am so tired by the evening that I struggle to feel good until I do this exercise. It is really valuable!

DO IT!

What did you do right today? Write it down or list it in your mind; just do it often enough to prove to yourself how often you do the right thing.

KEEPING THE NEEDY SPIRITS AT BAY

Coming across as needy is one of our biggest fears—and for a good reason: it kills opportunity. Overcoming it is so much easier said than done; believe me, I have felt needy for business more times than I would care to admit or remember. Knowing it comes with the territory does not make the pill any easier to swallow.

Neediness is selling just a little too hard (and where you're not coming from a place of sincere enthusiasm). It's putting product before relationship. It's pitching your wares before you even know much about the person you're talking to. It's shooting too soon before the other person knows, likes, and trusts you enough.

There are so many body language cues that can give it away. It might be talking too fast, saying "um" a lot, or failing to make enough eye contact. You might be wringing your hands unconsciously or swaying your body from side to side.

The tricky part is that we all develop relationships differently and don't know it! *We are not all created equal at establishing rapport with people.* Some people establish rapport quickly, while others take a bit longer. *Most people have good intentions, but we all have very varied skill levels at having others recognize those intentions.* You might want to read that last sentence again. It could be one reason why you are not getting the referral results you think you should be getting—others may not recognize the value that you think you're providing. That's one reason why some people have more success asking for referrals sooner than others.

We all know that we run and walk at different speeds. We can also accept that some people can carry a tune or draw better than we can because we saw it from an early age. The only gymnastics move I could ever do was a forward roll (a "roley poley" was what we called it in England)—these skill levels are clear to all. But when it comes to building a relationship, that's harder to measure and notice. Our poor evaluation skills in this area lead us to believe that we are superior to others when the reality is very debatable.

Part of it is believing that you are making a difference; this gives you confidence. Part of it comes from knowing your stuff; that builds confidence. My coaching clients also share with me that it makes a big difference to have a referral strategy. And the final part of it comes from hearing from others that you have made a difference!

Sometimes you have to fake not being needy. I know I have. Every once in a while, that's just part of being self-employed or working on commission. Incoming business is not a consistent machine that churns out exactly the same opportunities. You have to be an optimist to succeed, and sometimes that means painting a rosier picture than is the reality that day. This is not my favorite point to make because I do not like to suggest you should be insincere, but the business reality is that people don't want to come on board if they see the rats running away from a ship that looks like it's sinking!

Some People Will Never Get It

Remember the 20–60–20 percent? In light of the subject of this book, it may seem odd that I should have some kind of disclaimer here, but not everyone you meet is going to recommend you. I've been in many a meeting with a client of mine who is frustrated about someone who is not forthcoming with referrals.

There are too many dynamics and intangibles at work in human relationships to be able to figure everything out or to insist that you have a 100 percent success rate. As an optimist I do believe that some people who are initially wary can be warmed up and coached as they see the value and get to know, like, and trust you more. Nonetheless, don't resist too hard. You'll live longer being a tree that stays rooted but that gives a little when the wind blows.

HOW TO SLAY YOUR FEARS OF ASKING

Rarely a day goes by in my life as a referral coach when someone doesn't express the fear of coming across as pushy. Ever have this concern? If so, you're certainly not alone. *Many people say they are afraid to ask for referrals because they do not want to come across as pushy.* Yet I have never met anyone who had that fear who actually was a pushy individual. Have you? People who are really pushy are usually too blind to notice how they barge their way through life pressuring others to get what they want. And they are too insecure to admit it.

It's time to knock "pushy" on the head. Ready? Here are 10 strategies that will move you along.

1. SLAY THE MYTHICAL BEAST CALLED "PUSHY"

Walk through your last week and think of all the businesses you went into and people who called you: the bank, the dry cleaners, the coffee shop, the clothing store, the veterinarian, the bookstore. What percentage of all the retail people and salespeople you encountered were aggressive? Pause for a moment and really think hard.

How many tried to ram a product or service down your throat or upsell you to death? You know; they were *pushy*.

Any? I hardly ever have this experience. Sure, I get salespeople calling on me, but they're not bugging me if I've told them no or not now. Almost all of them give up after leaving *one* message!

Part of slaying the "pushy" beast is distinguishing between being assertive and being aggressive. I remember driving through central Iowa once (where let's just say the scenery is not very distracting) listening to a Brian Tracy audio and being startled by a distinction he made between the words *Passive*, *Assertive*, and *Aggressive*.

Many people confuse *assertive* with *aggressive*, and yet they could not be more different. Both aggression and passivity are based in low self-confidence. Nobody walks away from an aggressive person feeling good. Being aggressive is being pushy, obnoxious, annoying, and loud and is rooted in low self-worth.

Conversely, being assertive is healthy. It's asking for what you want because you believe someone else will truly be better off because of your product or service.

It's asking for a free glass of water when you're thirsty. It's interrupting a conversation between two people in a coffee shop to see if you can plug in your computer by their table. That is not pushy. Avoid confusing the two.

So to repeat my observation from before, I have never met anyone who told me he or she was afraid of being pushy who actually was! How about you?

Think about someone you know that you consider pushy. Is that how you run your business? Do you get feedback from people telling you that you're being pushy on a regular basis?

ASK YOURSELF: WHAT'S THE WORST THAT CAN HAPPEN IF I ASK FOR REFERRALS?

Is that outcome really so bad? If you didn't have the business, or date, or job, before you asked and you don't have it after, you've not lost anything.

So don't be afraid of rejection. It's a concept that holds no merit. You are not any worse off by asking and then hearing no (since you didn't have it before you asked either).

As ice hockey great Wayne Gretzky said, "You miss 100 percent of the shots you never take."

So, please, take a reality check. Like most of our fears, this one is almost always imagined.

It's Not All about You

Finally, people are not spending their day thinking about you, your call, or your referral request. Remember, people think about themselves 95 percent of the time, not you. Brian Tracy notes, "Never do or refrain from doing something because you are concerned about what people might think about you. The fact is that nobody is even thinking about you at all."

If all else fails, remember the 18/40/60 rule:

- When you're 18 years old, you are always worried about what others think of you.
- When you're 40, you don't care what others think of you.
- When you're 60, you realize nobody's been thinking about you the whole time!

2. Understand Why You Don't Always Ask for What You Want

In *The Aladdin Factor*, Jack Canfield and Mark Victor Hansen identify five possible reasons why people don't ask for what they want, further reinforcing the notion that the fear of being pushy is the product of ignorance and error. Here's what they found:

1. **Ignorance.** You don't know one or more of the following: what to ask for, whom to ask, when to ask, or how to ask.

2. **Mistaken beliefs.** *Example*: I don't want to be seen as pushy or needy. It's not pushy or needy if you genuinely believe you can help others whom this person cares about.

3. **Fear.** Fear is in control, especially the fear of rejection and the fear of looking foolish. Instead of taking action, Canfield and Hansen note, "We sit in judgment of others who are getting what they want." Also, asking can make us feel vulnerable and that's not comfortable! (See the section "Get Comfortable Getting Uncomfortable" in Chapter 3.)

4. **Pride.** We think we should be able to figure it out for ourselves. "We are a nation of loners and self-sufficient do-it-yourselfers who will stoically suffer in silence to the end."

5. **Low self-esteem.** According to Canfield, two in three adults suffer from low self-esteem. On those days when you're not feeling good about yourself, it's very hard to have the confidence to ask others to recommend you. If this sounds like you right now, do not accept this situation any longer—not least because your asking won't be effective and you won't get many more referrals! Check the Bibliography for resources that can help, start taking small steps, and work with a coach or counselor. If you don't have a high enough opinion of yourself, you're making it easy to take on the assumption that you're not worth helping.

3. GET UNDER YOUR OWN SKIN

Find ways to get some leverage on yourself. Ask someone else to hold you accountable for what you say you're going to do. It's one reason why high achievers hire a coach.

One of my favorite quotations comes from an interview that Peter Thomson had with Barry Hearn, who organizes major sporting events and manages professional athletes in the United Kingdom. Imagine an important meeting in your mind and say this to yourself:

Why did you start doing what you're doing? Did you not begin with a dream? Did you not once want to be in the position that you're in now? All your life you've aimed toward a certain point. Are you going to blow it now by not believing in yourself when it's your whole life? How much do you want this?

Here are some great questions to ask yourself:

♦ "Why should I hide my value from people who could benefit from it?"

♦ "Why am I denying my prospects a great opportunity?"

In other words, you are robbing the world of the contributions you can make!

And if you can't believe any of this, you should find something else you can get passionate about. You can't fake it.

4. BELIEVE IN YOURSELF, YOUR COMPANY, AND YOUR PRODUCT OR SERVICE

You are worthy of their referrals, okay? Part of people feeling awkward is when they don't believe in or use the product they're selling. *The more enthusiastic you are about what you do, the more success you will have.*

Learn from a 19-year-old. In Cameron Johnson's autobiography, *You Call the Shots*, he explains his philosophy that made him a multimillionaire before he hit 20. "My feeling is, I'd be doing my customers a disservice if I let them NOT buy my product. I'm always genuinely fascinated to know why people WOULDN'T want what I'm selling."

Many people will still not be interested, but that does not make you pushy.

5. LIKE YOURSELF MORE AND MORE

Liking yourself is another huge factor that makes the feeling of being pushy much less of a concern. Obviously this is a process for anyone. How important is it?

How much you like yourself is going to dictate what you ask for. Why? Because if you think you deserve to help big fish, you will continue to move in that direction. You will make sure you have the knowledge and skill. You will fish where the fish are and not spend any more time at chamber events or business mixers for start-ups. You will even work on yourself more to overcome ghosts from the past until you believe you do deserve the finer things. You will surround yourself with more positive and motivated people.

"If not me, then who?" will become your mindset too.

6. BE WILLING TO FAIL

The road to fulfilling your potential includes asking others for what you want. This also includes hearing people say no to you. (See the section "Overcome the Biggest Myth in Our Culture" in Chapter 3.)

I did give up on myself once in business just a few months after I first started in 2002. It was a book that got me back on track. *Roadtrip Nation* (by Mike Marriner, Nathan Gebhard, and Joanne Gordon) told the stories of 30 highly accomplished people.

As I looked over my notes after I'd read it, I was struck by how most of the people said something like "Failure is inevitable and necessary" and "You must develop a powerful relationship with failure." I remember being so surprised at how often this came up and asking myself, "How come nobody ever taught me that it's normal to fail and that you have to pick yourself up again?" (And maybe people did and I wasn't listening.)

I still carry around those notes every day in my planner. And there have been many days since then when I have needed those reminders.

This is incredibly important. There is no shortcut. Whatever you need to do to truly engrain this fact, do it! Start by committing to one act of courage each day.

7. KNOW HOW TO BOUNCE BACK

It's up to you to develop a mindset that helps you bounce back from inevitable rejection and unreturned phone calls. Have a snap response to put your mind back into the positive (or at least neutral) position. When it happens to me, I just hang up and say, "She doesn't get it!" or "He is totally missing the boat!" or "Their business must be going down the tubes." I remember asking Nate McCardell, a sales manager I know, what he said to himself as a successful producer when he was turned down. But I can't print what he said! The gist was that those people had severe cognitive challenges.

I also like the expression SWSWSWSW: some will, some won't, so what, someone's waiting. It's a helpful phrase that describes the real world. There are plenty of opportunities out there if you follow the effective strategies of people who have truly had success; tweak them only a little, as necessary, and persist.

The reality is that 80 percent of the people you interact with won't do business with you for one reason or another, and if you can't handle that, you've made an interesting career choice! I believe that most people avoid that 80 percent like the plague and so are not asking much for business or referrals and blame it on not wanting to come across as the "typical pushy salesperson" that is mostly a figment of their imagination.

It doesn't really matter what you say to yourself so long as it helps you persist and deal with the challenging reality.

8. Know What You Want and Be Specific When You Ask!

This is Step 3 in the referral conversation (more on this in Chapter 6). You can do everything right, but if you then say, "Well, if you can think of someone else I should talk with, please have him or her give me a call!" you'll get few referrals. That's because such a request is too vague—the average person has dozens of people swirling around their thoughts at any given time. You want to make it as easy as possible for others to know what you want by either naming a name or identifying a small group of people to whom this person can easily endorse you.

If you are not clear enough, others are unlikely to put in the time to figure out what you want. That's your job.

9. Take Action

Take action in spite of your fears. Practice finding a way to ask that gets more comfortable with time—small steps outside your comfort zone.

To prompt yourself to move forward, ask yourself, "What is the best that could happen?"

Focus your mind on what the *benefits* are to the person you're asking. How *does* that person benefit? One study I read found that 85 percent of relationships were *improved* by making a referral. Maintain eye contact when you ask. Smile. Be respectful.

10. Try Humor

Humor can be *very* effective when it's authentic.

One client of mine, who had not been given a choice about attending my seminar, told me that he'd told a trusted client very sincerely, "Yeah, my boss made me take this referral class, and now we're supposed to be asking everyone for referrals." After they'd had a good laugh at my expense, he got a great referral—an invitation to attend the annual convention of this person's trade association that October and get numerous personal introductions to prospects. Why was this person willing to do it? "Because I know you're not going to give anyone the hard sell."

Another client of mine told one of her clients, "I know you've mentioned your two brothers before. I expect when you get together for baseball games, you spend most of the time talking about the beneficiaries on your life insurance policies [they laugh]. While I don't expect you to know their exact situation, do you think they might be open to a quick conversation with me some time?"

Sam Morton of 21st Century Media, a successful U.K. filmmaker I interviewed a few years ago, shared that he transitioned to asking for referrals by saying, "In my shameless business development mode, would you be willing to recommend me to those other two contacts you mentioned?"

These 10 strategies can help you make huge shifts in your business and your life by helping you learn to ask with more courage and ultimately see asking as a fun opportunity to help others. Only your actions will make a difference though, so start today by asking for something specific that will move you forward toward your goals.

MAKE ASKING A HABIT AND PREPLAN YOUR ASKS

I wanted to share something I have been doing that is a wonderfully effective referral habit and a best practice from one of my role models.

Every Saturday I do my weekly planning (see Chapter 7), and I have about 30 habits that I go through to make sure I am prepared and on top of things for the upcoming week.

One of the habits is something that's recommended by motivational speaker and author Jack Canfield. He strongly advises asking yourself the question, "What would I love to ask this person?" He swears by it as being a highly successful approach for him, and we all know we should do what successful people do if we want to get the same results they get.

As I look ahead to every meeting I have, I ask myself that question. Options include asking the person for business, a referral, or a speaking opportunity or asking the person to consider purchasing my new DVD or CD. The list can be endless. (For other ideas on what to ask for, also see "Start with Your Like List" in Chapter 5.)

Some time ago I got together with Susan, someone I met years ago who's made more significant changes in her life than anyone else I've ever known personally. For the same reason I am following Canfield's advice, I sought answers from Susan. I wondered what had helped her make such profound changes. My "ask" from her was broad: "What have you done in recent years that has helped you become so successful?"

Susan recommended the Landmark Forum class offered by Landmark Education, which she said had helped her make some powerful breakthroughs in her life. I knew there were a couple of areas in my life where I was not getting the results I wanted on my own, and so I decided I should do the same. I went back home, went online, and signed up immediately. Little did I know how profound that decision would be!

Ask Consistently

Asking consistently must become a habit if you are to expect great results. Schedule the time to do it *and* come up with an answer to "What would I love to ask him or her for?" It *is* that simple.

IT'S OK TO START SMALL

If you want to ease into this, start by asking for people's e-mail addresses or mailing addresses for your newsletter or for birthday cards. You could ask the person to attend your networking group as a guest, or you might ask for introductions to other centers of influence—and there's a soft way to do that. If you want to meet the person's CPA, you ask, "Can you recommend a good accountant?" People will tell you whether that accountant is good or not. They will not recommend someone if they're not impressed.

If they say good things about the individual, respond by saying, "That would be a good person for me to know because if he and I work together, we can probably meet your needs better. Would you mind shooting him an e-mail and just suggest that you think it would be a good idea if he and I got together some time? Thanks."

While it's okay to start small, don't plan to stay there long if you'd like to stay in business.

ONLY ASK IF THERE'S WATER IN THE WELL

You must make emotional bank account deposits in order to have earned the right to ask. Otherwise you will feel awkward and hurt the relationship.

DON'T ASK THE SAME PERSON EVERY TIME YOU SEE HIM OR HER

That would get annoying. You'll know too; it won't feel right.

ASKING MORE OFTEN MEANS GIVING MORE OFTEN

Read that again! What's great about this habit is you have to think harder about what *you* are bringing to the table. You can't ask if you haven't done anything for the person lately! You have to keep adding value to the relationship by asking yourself the question, "How can I most add value to this person?"

You are forced to do a better job and keep raising the bar, or else you really can't keep asking. This is such a great win-win for the relationship, and it keeps you on your toes. In addition, it keeps the relationship from getting too comfortable.

BE SPECIFIC WHEN YOU ASK

Don't ask for "more money." Ask for "$5,000." Don't ask for referrals to "anyone" the person thinks might benefit. Ask to meet "Michelle Gonzalez, the VP at First National Bank." (See Chapter 6 for more on this.)

EXPECT TO GET WHAT YOU ASK FOR

I admit this one takes some practice, but I promise you it makes a big difference in what you say and how confidently you communicate.

A powerful way to practice this is to role-play. First you ask as if you are sure the person will say no. Get feedback on the words you used, your tone of voice, and your body language.

Then do it again knowing the person will say yes and get feedback on that too. It's a terrific way to get clear about how you're thinking and creating obstacles in your path.

PERSISTENCE PAYS

Keep asking!

I would love to hear some stories from you about successes you get from simply making asking a habit. I cannot urge you more strongly to truly turn this into a habit if it is not already. Most people wing it, and that is not for you. May this bring you much joy!

DO IT!

Put 10 minutes in your schedule to preplan your asks each week. Combine this with Step 3 of the Six-Step Fearless Referral Conversation (see Chapter 6).

It's How You Ask for Referrals

A referral request should focus on helping others, not on growing your business.

As often as possible, word your referral request in a way for clients to focus on the value they got and how that might also help people they care about. *It's almost* never *about you! The wording must focus on helping other people that matter to your client.*

Avoid lines like:

- "I get paid in two ways."
- "I grow my business by referrals and was wondering who else you think I should talk to."
- "I am trying to increase my business and would like your help."

Avoid the "me, me, me" approach. It turns people off and sounds needy. (The exceptions to this: These lines only work on occasion with sympathetic family members and very close friends. Also, if you have been in business for a long time and have excellent relationships, you

99

can ask for help and get results—it's counterintuitive but works. You have enough emotional bank account deposits to pull this off.)

It is more effective to appeal to what matters in the life of your client than to hope he or she is deeply concerned with seeing your business succeed.

Really, when you left your last dental appointment, did you spend any time the rest of the day fretting about whether the dentist was still going to be in business the next time you went back for a cleaning? What are the last few restaurants you visited? Has the thought ever crossed your mind that they might not be there in a month, and so you need to take action to help?

Think about most of the businesses you patronize. If they don't ask you for referrals (and I'm sure most of them don't), how much time do you spend thinking of other people you should recommend them to? It's almost a ridiculous question, and yet that's exactly what this book is designed to address and why there's such a need for it. Almost no one is doing it well!

DO IT!

Think about how you are currently asking for your referrals. Is the language you use all about you or all about them?

DON'T SHOOT TOO SOON

Before explaining when is the best time to ask for a referral, here are a few words on when not to ask.

This isn't a science. Sometimes people's discomfort with asking comes from knowing the relationship isn't strong or they really haven't brought much value. I was sitting with a financial advisor this week who was telling me he rarely asked during an early appointment with a client. Wanting to hear *him* tell me, I asked him why not. He said, "I haven't brought much value. I wouldn't recommend me at that point!"

NEW FINANCIAL AND INSURANCE SERVICE REPS BE WARNED

Many new financial and insurance service reps shoot too soon. They are often trained to ask right away because getting referrals is so important. Unfortunately most of their client relationships are not strong enough from a business credibility standpoint to earn referrals, and so it creates awkwardness on both sides and rejection; and sooner rather than later, the reps give up because it feels wrong. They are tired of getting a bloody nose. Ironically, many reps probably give up right around the time they should start asking!

New sales reps need to be trained on exceeding expectations and consistently adding more value. They need to be asking themselves, "What can I do to be more liked and trusted by this person?" They also need to believe that they are in the helping business, not the selling business.

ESTABLISH BUSINESS CREDIBILITY

You can ask friends or family for help, but they too will usually need to know you're quickly becoming competent. People are understandably wary about putting their integrity on the line when integrity is the foundation upon which our character and values are based. That's the power of a word-of-mouth endorsement.

Unfortunately when you are starting out, client relationships are seldom strong enough from a business credibility standpoint to earn referrals. If you are a new salesperson, you are likely meeting with people who may know you well and trust you on a personal level, but often they do not have a lot of confidence in you professionally. Your prospect may still have you labeled as the kid down the street who used to mow the lawn or may think of you in terms of what you did in a previous career. I know when I first started my business, my family still had me pegged as a teacher somehow "playing" at something else for a while. It took about four years and a postcard from a speaking engagement 1,000 miles from my home before they started taking me seriously!

So what do you do if you are new? Diffuse these concerns by explaining how much you are learning and how much expertise you have at your fingertips and by laying out your goals for the grand future you see before you. Talk as though success for you is simply a matter of time. Confidence is a magnet.

Do Not Ask at Every Meeting You Have

It is always wise to have referrals on your mind. It is always wise to plant seeds about referrals.

It is *not* wise to ask for referrals every time you see people. You will get annoying. And people will not go to bat for you unless they are sure that you have done a great job. Any names you get will be mostly worthless, and those people will not return your calls.

DO IT!

Whenever you're in doubt, ask yourself, "If I had to give this relationship a grade, what would it be? What do I need to do to get this relationship to a B+ or an A? How else can I add value to this person?" (Often this will not relate to your business.) Then you'll be ready to ask and get what you ask for.

The Right Time to Ask and the Best Time to Ask for Referrals

It's all about value. Remember, referrals must be earned! The right time to ask is simply when your client is happiest.

During a Formal Meeting with a Client

Within a structured meeting, have a conversation with your client that solicits some positive feedback. If what you hear sounds like you have done a good job, you should have a green light to ask about other people you could help too. Use the Six-Step Fearless Referral Conversation (see Chapter 6).

On the Phone

As you talk with your clients on the phone, inquire about some value you added to him or her; then ask for a referral. Give first. Then receive.

The other person's guard is down because you have another reason to call that adds value to him or her. You are building the relationship further.

I would urge you to rack your brain and think of as many creative ways as possible to call people and make emotional bank account deposits. It could easily be to follow up on value you added in another way—a referral you sent or some sales ideas you e-mailed.

This isn't just some technique. The relationship has to be there. Let me repeat. The relationship has to be there! You can't forward one e-newsletter to that person and call expecting instant referrals. People will see right through any ruse. But if you truly care about that person and make deposits, those referral requests get easier.

103

Here's an example of what you might say on a call:

Step 1. Give. "Crystal, I'm calling for two reasons. First, I was curious how things worked out with (my referral to you) Nicole?"

Crystal responds that things worked out well.

"Good! I'm glad that worked out. I thought you two would connect and find some areas to be able to help each other."

Step 2. Get. "The other reason I'm calling is that I wanted to ask you, how well do you know Sondra Hicks? Would you be willing to put in a good word for me with her, because I have been helping a lot of executives in similar situations. Really all you need to do is tell her that I specialize in working with executive teams and that you'd recommend that she at least have a quick conversation with me; then just find out if I can give her a call some time."

Ask Over a Meal

It could be during a lunch, coffee, or beer meeting where you have provided value. All the same rules apply as above.

Listen to Your Gut

Sometimes you just know you've established good rapport and can ask for what you want. This sense usually develops with experience.

The Best Way to Say Thank You

Step 2 of the Six-Step Fearless Referral Conversation (see Chapter 6) helps you determine if you've brought value and earned the referral. If it's obvious at other times, great! The only situation in which I'd suggest waiting until later in the meeting is if it seems too off topic during a meeting that is meant to focus on your client.

Note: You can add value early, often, and on occasion, but early in the relationship can sometimes be the best time to ask! Why? Because you have given your client something that's truly worth talking about!

A past client of mine in California, Jenna, is one exception to the rule about not asking too soon. She does such a great job at creating a wow first impression that she gets most of her referrals early on in her client relationships. This happens because her financial planning process is truly holistic and is one her clients have never experienced before—so they talk about it to others. Also she is a master at managing the experience by offering fresh-baked chocolate chip cookies and serving gourmet coffee in china cups.

Here's another example. Recently I switched chiropractors—I'm on my fifth. I've seen four over the past 16 years with fair-to-disappointing results. My new chiropractor, Corinne, takes a holistic approach (I was a little skeptical about what exactly that meant) and does far more than simply adjust my back. She spends most of the time working on my ligaments and muscles that support the adjustments. She also discusses nutrition and specific exercises and explains how the events in our lives manifest themselves in our bodies as physical symptoms. One of the first things she told me was that her goal was not to have to see me more than a few times—the exact opposite of what I've heard from every other chiropractor.

I felt so dramatically different and better after just that first appointment that I raved about her to three people that same day. What's scary is that just a week later I was already used to feeling that much better, and so it was no longer a daily talking point. In other words, sometimes the best time to leverage a referral is early and often—but only after you have earned it with such an impressive first experience.

THE BEST TIME TO ASK IS AFTER
THE MEETING IS OVER

Dave was a client of mine who wanted to work with more veterinarians. He had one such client up to that point, and was having lunch with the office manager of that clinic. His first request was that she call other clinics in the area to recommend the workshop he had done on disability insurance, but she looked uncomfortable about doing that. So he dropped the topic and they talked about other things.

As he was sitting in his car with the door open about to say goodbye, he transitioned back to his referral request: "Gail, what *would* be the best way to find out how I might be able to help some of the other vets around here?"

She thought for a moment and said: "Aren't you having a booth at our convention in a couple of months?"

He said he was, and so she came up with the idea, "Well, why don't I introduce you to some people then?" The quality of his referral opportunity went from asking for a warmed-up call (50 percent) to a personal introduction (80 percent)!

The story got better. Two months later, it turned out that Gail was presenting at the convention, and as she wrapped up, she told her audience, "And if you ever want a great workshop for your clinic on disability insurance, talk to Dave Edmundson over there. He did a terrific job for us!" Close to 30 people gave him their contact information.

I like the time after a meeting to ask because the other person is more relaxed. The meeting is over, you know you've done a good job, and you've transitioned the conversation. Now you're talking about what that person is doing over the weekend or discussing some other safe personal topic that's not upsetting to him or her.

Then you pivot back to business:

Step 1

"Oh by the way, when we were talking earlier, you'd mentioned" (and now you get specific):

a.   "… speaking at a company event"

b.   "… that your parents live nearby"

c.   "… that you thought your business partner might benefit from doing the kind of work we've been doing"

d.   "… that your cousin was moving to the area

Step 2

a.   "How would you recommend setting up something like that?"

b.   "What would be the best way to find out if they'd be open to a quick conversation with me sometime?"

c.   "Do you think the three of us should have lunch sometime?"

d.   "Do you think she might be open to me connecting with her about her real estate needs and search?"

DO IT!

I know this last step is a technique. However, it works for a reason, and it works when your request is sincere. Look at your upcoming meetings for the week with people where there is water in the well. What would you love to ask these people? Preplan your ask. After the formal meeting is over, transition the conversation to something light and personal. Make your referral request after this when you are on your way out either to the door, to your car, or to the elevator.

CHAPTER 5

Fearless Referral-Getting Strategies

The step from knowing to doing is rarely taken.

—Ralph Waldo Emerson

Where Does Your Referral Business Come From?

Three years ago, I was having coffee in Worcester, England, with a man named Richard, then a director of the G.M.G., an organization that hired me to do a couple of referral seminars for its members—all small business owners in synergistic industries. While talking to him about his own company over the previous few weeks, I had asked him three questions. He told me that his answers had helped him enormously in determining where he wanted to focus for that upcoming year. Perhaps they'll help you, too.

DO IT!

Go though these three questions so you can make sure you focus on your referral sources better.

QUESTION 1

Where exactly has all your business come from over the past 12 months?

Richard knew he was getting most of his business from referrals, but he was startled to see that in the past three years *all* his business had come from referrals.

Identifying specifically who has recommended you is a helpful reality check. Some professionals and clients you know may well be ones you like a great deal and even enjoy spending business time with, but they are not actually helping your business grow. You need to be aware of who these people are.

Conversely, there are quiet-spoken individuals who are out there endorsing you, and you are barely noticing.

QUESTION 2

Who are your top referral sources?

What also surprised Richard was that it was only 10 percent of his clients who had referred him business in the past three years (along with some other centers of influence). He had never asked any of them for referrals even though he'd been in business for more than 25 years. As I dug to find out if he'd done anything to find referrals, he did say that he told stories to clients to "drop hints" about other companies he wanted to do business with.

For example, if he was talking with a happy client who knew the owner of the BMW dealership, he would mention how he was working with the owner of the Audi dealership in the hope that his client would connect the dots. I am sure there are occasions when this helped. However, the numbers don't lie: 10 percent!

The real points here are:

- How many of your clients are you asking?

- If you're not, why not?

- What are you going to do differently over the next three months to improve the relationships you have so that you can ask confidently and comfortably?

- What are you doing to keep your top referral relationships strong and flourishing?

QUESTION 3

Why are they your top referral sources?

This was also a revelation to Richard. "I noticed from looking at the names that my top referral sources were almost all projects with overseas companies, and that I had spent lots of time with these people. Lots of quality time on planes, at their offices and over meals. It was the personal connection we made on these projects. The 10 percent are the ones I got along best with. We became friends." Remember the Likeability Factor? Richard was getting referred by the companies that had gotten to know him better and realized what a great guy he was.

What a huge discovery!

Step 2 for Richard was to then ask himself, "How can I spend more time with my clients and do less work virtually so they can get to know me better as a person? *How can I find more ways to be face-to-face with my clients to build those relationships?*"

Can you relate to that one?

The next question *you'll* be asking yourself is, "What am I doing in my working relationships that I should also be doing when I want to connect better with others?" To answer this, you'll need to take part in a little exercise. The next time you are engaged in a conversation with a client who has successfully referred you to others, ask the following:

♦ **"How did I come up in the conversation?"** You want to know what people are talking about so you know what the hot-button topics are and so you can coach others better.

♦ **"I'm curious: what did you share with Fiona when you recommended me?"** This will help you find out what wording works for you to get referrals.

Question 3 is vital, and so it's essential that you do this exercise so that you can give yourself an honest response to it. Who gives you the most business and why? What difference did you make with that referral source that the person likes you so much to refer you? The truth is most likely that you gave first before you received and that you likely gave a great deal.

Here's how I developed one of my first great referral sources:

Tim was a new insurance agent when I met him in a leads group. His wife was pregnant with their first child, and he was working hard in his business and not getting his desired results. He was putting in 12-to-14-hour days and was questioning what he was doing wrong. His confidence was at an all-time low. So that's what we addressed first. I told him to identify the time in his life when he was most confident—what was he doing in all areas of his life and what else made that time so memorable? We also talked about physiology and how we carry ourselves during times of struggles compared with times of great confidence.

The time Tim hit upon (and by the way, it rarely takes long for people to know when this time was) was a specific year in college when he had his own radio show and had asked out Ann, the woman he married. Music had been really important to him at that point in his life. He realized that he had been shutting that out as if it weren't somehow appropriate now that he was a business owner.

The changes he made immediately included leaving his office and sitting in his car to play a fun tune whenever something happened that really frustrated him. He put pictures on his desk of the ultrasounds of Ann and their daughter. He started keeping a journal of what he was grateful for; I still remember him telling me about a Vietnam veteran that was in his office who had a very rough life since the war and how his own struggles paled by comparison. He quickly became aware of his body language and posture. He started walking with more confidence, keeping his chin elevated and his shoulders back. He focused on his body language in client meetings by sitting forward and listening intently. Clients could sense the confidence, and therefore he began to sell more ... to the tune of doubling his agency's production.

We also came up with new business strategies, and his numbers continued to grow. Within nine months, he not only became a father, but also became a Top 100 agent, a prestigious award for new agents in the largest car insurance company in the country. Within three years he was managing new agents elsewhere in the country, showing them how to run an effective business. Since then, he has been promoted twice more.

Some of my best referral sources are people I met at pivotal stages in their business, either early on or when their frustration level was to the point where they knew they had to make some positive changes. I am sure you will find the same—that you met certain clients at a crucial time in their lives and therefore they really appreciate how you helped them. For others, it may be specific ways you excelled in providing customer service and treating your customers—all things you can replicate with all your clients once you're aware of what they are and how powerful they are. A client of mine got referrals this past holiday season from top clients by personally taking gift baskets to them. Obviously he'll do something next year to impress them as much.

START WITH YOUR "LIKE LIST"

One of the best ways to jump-start getting more referrals is to do what I recommend to all the people I coach when we start working together: put together a Like List.

Why is this so important? Because almost all your best referrals will come from people who like you a lot—even if that's only because you brought them great results. The more people like you, the more they will go to bat for you. Make it easier for youself to get results. Remember Robert Cialdini's Rule of Liking says that when people like you, they want to say yes to you (see Chapter 1).

So leverage the best people (arguably the low-hanging fruit) and make it easy for them. *This means you must be crystal clear about what you are asking for—so clear that the person you're asking doesn't have to think about whom you want to meet.*

1. Take 20 minutes and write a list of all the people who like you the most. It will likely be very similar to a list of people you like the most!

2. Write down what you would like to ask those people for.

3. Once you have the names and the information you requested, then the only decision is to determine how you want to ask to maximize the chances you'll get a yes. Face-to-face is usually better, not least because it's harder for people to say no!

DO IT!

Putting together a Like List is one of the actions I would recommend more than almost any other in the book as somewhere to start.

As you work your way through Step 2 in the list on the previous page, your first tendency may well be to think about doing business with each person you've written down. That's a perfectly good option (see the final point below). I would also urge you to think bigger and more creatively than this:

♦ Perhaps your contact works for a company whose employees could use your help.

♦ Maybe he or she is on a team or in a department that would be a better request.

♦ Perhaps you could ask to interview that person because he or she belongs to a target market that would be a great niche for your business.

♦ Could you ask for an introduction to one of the person's centers of influence since that person could open up new doors for you?

♦ What about a possible speaking opportunity to do a workshop?

♦ Or maybe this person networks in a powerhouse organization that you would love to be invited to as his or her guest.

Don't just think about immediate business. Many of these ideas could bring you far more revenue in the long term.

Remember, people are more defensive when they think you are targeting them. Often you are more likely to get business with a person by telling stories about the work you have done and how you have helped others like that person. It is innate for people to personalize what they are hearing, so as you describe clients who are happy because you helped them with something, your listeners are going to be thinking about themselves. (They will think about themselves provided that they see themselves as being in a similar situation. It wouldn't work to tell a new business owner how you help affluent physicians. The business owner will think you're talking about a different species.)

Last year, a client of mine called a couple of his friends from his Like List who were veterinarians. His "ask" was for their advice on how to target-market that profession. He spent quite a bit of time explaining to them how he helped vets with managing their finances and protecting their businesses. By the end of the conversation, both of them blurted out, "Gosh, David, it sounds like I really should meet with you too!"

Ask an Expert

When deciding how to best ask for a referral, the Ask the Expert option (see Chapter 6 for more details) is an effective strategy. When you are talking to your contact, ask, "What would be the best way to find out if this is something that might be valuable to the other partners in your firm, or in your industry?"

If you're not currently using this question, you're missing out. It works extremely well with people who like you so long as you ask in a sincere, curious way.

Do Business Together

Even if it's not what you're asking for now, make it an ultimate goal to have your Ask the Expert contacts be clients if they aren't already. Why? They know your work well, and that makes it easier for them to endorse you. A referral is usually more compelling when you can say you are a client too. It's similar to the concept of you selling a product you use yourself versus trying to sell a product you don't use. The credibility is higher.

My insurance agent finds it very easy to send business to his Realtor center of influence when he tells his customers, "If you don't have a Realtor that you trust, you should talk to Trent [shows them Trent's card]. He helped my wife and me find a home a couple of years ago. My wife, Erica, is pretty cynical and asks a lot of tough questions, and she thought he was great—so you don't even need to take my word for it! Would you be interested in hearing from him?"

LEVERAGING THE VIRTUAL WORLD

In this age of virtual communication the fact that 70 percent of our phone calls go to voice mail makes it tempting to resort to e-mail, texts, LinkedIn, and even Facebook and Twitter for most correspondence—including referral requests. I know that different generations seem to have different preferences about communication. How does this help and hinder your referral business?

According to Tim Burress, CEO of Get Control!, a firm that helps Fortune 500 companies better manage e-mail:

♦   The average U.S. resident receives 80 e-mails a day.

♦   One-fourth of all e-mails are deleted unread.

♦   Two-thirds are either incomplete or confusing *for the recipient.*

Given that technological advances are happening so quickly, techniques that work in social media will likely change. This is why I am not going to devote a section of this book to "10 tips for getting referrals from Facebook." Fortunately, the principles that will get you referrals from your network are going to be the same regardless of the medium.

I think there is some danger that virtual introductions can be somewhat weaker at present (we're almost all connected to some people

117

online that we barely know), but that too will likely change or become understood. Our credibility is still on the line.

Here are some thoughts that, I hope, are still current when you read this!

E-Mailing People Can Too Easily Be a Way to Avoid Being Rejected

E-mailing can be a crutch to avoid a real-time conversation. Do "gut checks" regularly to make sure you are e-mailing for all the right reasons. If a phone call is in order, pick up the phone and call! After all, do you know anyone who does not own a phone? People find it much harder to tell you no when you are face-to-face with them. They also find it harder to say no when you are on the phone because at least then you are a real person.

With e-mail, it seems we are treating people more and more as we do motorists on the road. Those motorists are not people with personalities that we hold open a door for; they are maniacs in speedy machines putting our lives at risk. They cease to be ordinary people with everyday challenges. It's the same as people who e-mail us. They become rabid salespeople interrupting our days, evenings, and weekends.

Please think hard about whether a phone call might not be more effective.

E-Mail Is Instantly Disposable

"Can you e-mail me something about that?" is almost now the modern-day equivalent of being pushed aside with a "Can you send me some information?" (which I will then throw away unopened as soon as it arrives).

From a referral standpoint, the best order is personal meeting, phone conference call, and then virtually: e-mail or LinkedIn—but they all work some of the time. When all you do is sum things up in your e-mail, don't be surprised when your message goes straight to its recipient's recycle bin.

E-MAIL IS LESS EFFECTIVE FOR PERSUADING OTHERS

Why? *Miscommunication is more likely.* The 15 studies cited in *YES!* by Goldstein, Martin, and Cialdini find six quite significant challenges with using e-mail compared with having a face-to-face or telephone conversation.

1. All the nonverbal cues (voice inflection and physical gestures) are missing. Remember, most of our communication is accomplished through either nonverbal (eye contact, gestures) means or the tone of our voice. A much smaller percentage is determined by the words we use. Ouch for e-mail!

2. The meaning of a message is harder to interpret—especially sarcasm, seriousness, anger, and sadness.

3. Senders of e-mail are usually unaware that a message can be misunderstood. We rarely take the time to reread our e-mails carefully before we send them. Even when we do, we seldom ask ourselves, "Could the person I'm sending this to interpret this content in a way I don't mean?" This issue is never going to get any easier given the growing volume of our in-boxes.

4. People are less likely to exchange personal information in an e-mail that helps to build rapport. No relationship, no referrals.

5. Women are even less persuaded by e-mail than men.

6. We are increasingly likely to be interacting with people from cultures and countries different from our own where being curt in our communication will hinder us further.

Mass E-Mailing for a Favor Rarely Works

Mass e-mails create a diffusion of responsibility so that nobody steps up to the plate. This kind of e-mailing is too impersonal. Individuals do not feel as if they are being addressed.

It's Easier for People to Put Off Your Virtual Request

We want to act consistently with our commitments and values. When people tell you to your face that they will follow through on a referral they've mentioned, they feel a much greater sense of obligation to do so. One of the six universal principles of influence is commitment and consistency, which will be further discussed in Chapter 6.

E-Mail Still Has Its Supporters

In fact, e-mail and other virtual communication are the preferred medium for quite a lot of people. We have to respect the fact that some people like the choice of when to respond and do not want more phone calls interrupting their day.

Virtual Warm-Ups

Virtual correspondence can be great for warming up referrals. Many of the clients I'm currently working with have success getting referral sources to warm up their referrals by e-mail (Step 5 in the Six Steps covered in the next chapter). Using a prewritten paragraph of what to say, with permission for them to change it however they see fit, can work pretty well, especially given how busy most people are (or think they are!) nowadays.

THE WEB AS A SOURCE FOR REFERRALS

LinkedIn, Google searches, and business Web sites can be good sources of possible referral requests. For more on this, see the next section. Personally, though, I still think that a combination of listening better and asking different questions feels more authentic most of the time for sourcing referral prospects.

DO IT!

If you are asking for a referral, do it in person whenever humanly possible or by phone. Use e-mail for coaching others how to introduce you.

FISH FOR REFERRALS BEFORE YOU ASK

How well do you "fish" for referrals? This is the opportunistic antennae you want to develop more and more.

STOP BEING SO VAGUE

One of the things that amazes me when I work with people on getting more referrals is how often I find people telling me that they don't know whom they want that specific client to introduce them to. This is Step 3 in my Six-step process (see Chapter 6). It's the most important step. I tend to hear vague responses like "Oh, other business owners they know" or "Some of their friends or neighbors—maybe some family members" or "I work better with women" (oh, you mean over 50 percent of the 300 million people in this country?). (This is, by the way, one more reason to have a target market—this will be covered in my second book.)

The reason I'm so surprised is that we're talking about your next possible piece of business. It doesn't work to say, "If you can think of others I should talk to, please have them give me a call." It rarely works to say, "Who else do you know that I should be talking to?" You've got to be more specific.

Your job is to narrow down your referral request to 2 or 3 people. Your clients are crazy busy just like everyone else. The odds of them spending time figuring out whom among the 200-plus people they know that they should introduce you to are very slim.

It is *your responsibility* to identify specific people you'd like to be referred to. Only a few raving fans will do it for you.

Listen for Opportunities

You belong to one of two types of people when it comes to hearing referral opportunities:

♦ One group will have one ear to the ground, listening for other business opportunities.

♦ The other group is 100 percent focused on the task at hand, and any such opportunities go in one ear and out the other.

This is not a criticism, but *if you fall into the second group and you do not know other people your clients know, it's time to get more curious. You are missing out on the chance to help a lot of people and do more business.*

One of the comments I've heard from many of my clients on this topic is "I'm just listening differently now," and as a result, they are hearing more people mentioned who might be referral request possibilities.

YOUR JOB IS TO FISH USING "FORD" AND TO MAKE THIS A HABIT

You've got to take a few minutes here and there to inquire about other people in their lives. FORD is an acronym I heard about from the Ninja Selling program for Realtors.

F: *Family and friends.* Who do they spend free time with? Who are they close to?

O: *Occupation.* Who do they work closely with at their company? Who are their best clients? What synergistic professionals do they work closely with? Who are the primary suppliers to their industry? Where do they get their new business?

R: *Recreation and hobbies.* What activities and organizations are they involved in?

D: *Dreams and goals.* What do they hope to accomplish in the next 12 months? What plans are they making for the future?

Some of this research can be done before meetings, perhaps by your assistant. Does the person have a business Web site that may mention others the person works with and top clients or industries he or she specializes in? What people is he or she connected to on LinkedIn? Google the person's name and see what comes up.

If your memory is like most people's, write down the information you've found. It will always be helpful for conversation in the future and tells your client that you cared enough to remember.

LEVERAGE THE "LIKING" AND "COMFORT" FACTORS

The Liking and Comfort Factors provide excellent opportunities to garner referrals.

LIKING

Listen for how much your client likes a certain person when the client talks about that person. If you can hear in the client's voice that the client is not too fond of, say, his or her boss, how do you think it's going to be for your client to want to refer you to that person?

If your client tells you that you should talk to someone in the HR department, you might want to find out who the client likes the most in HR even if it that person may not be the decision maker. Your advocate will get you a warmer referral, and because you're leveraging strong relationships, your end result will be much more favorable.

If you're using LinkedIn, make sure to say, "I noticed you're connected to these three people on LinkedIn. How well do you know them, because these are precisely the type of people I can help the most."

It is common sense: if someone likes you, he or she is more likely to help you out.

COMFORT

It's critical to ask yourself not only "Who do I want the client to introduce me to?" but also "Who would this client be more comfortable referring me to?"

We have to think about what types of conversations real people actually have and how we can incorporate what we do into that. It's our responsibility. If our referral source doesn't know what to say to introduce us, he or she is not going to say anything. Now, there's nothing wrong with asking for your client's guidance on this.

If you are a financial advisor, would your client be more comfortable discussing ways you can help coworkers in a professional business setting, or their family? Some families don't talk about money or insurance with each other. Others know it is a vital topic to discuss. Your job is deciding which direction to take that referral conversation by playing detective a little and getting a sense of what your client would be more willing to do.

These two factors matter so much because the more they work in your favor, the easier it is for your referral source to recommend you.

If you want more referrals, you must fish as often as humanly possible. It's your next piece of business, and if you're doing a good job and your client likes you, you've got someone right there who can help you.

IT WOULD BE SILLY OF YOU NOT TO SAY THIS

If you want nonthreatening wording that makes it easy to transition a conversation for you to ask for what you want, here is something that works fabulously. It fits with asking for anything—a referral, an appointment, and more business.

I use this wording whenever I'm talking to people I believe I can help professionally. I tell them, *"You know, it would be silly of me not to mention* that I specialize in working with *insurance and financial professionals* [people who do what you do] and helping them get more referrals." Usually then I'll ask them some questions about their referral business to see if they are interested (since I've never met anyone I couldn't help—have you?).

A testimonial: Ken, a very successful referral coaching client of mine, was expressing how he still felt a little uncomfortable sometimes approaching some of the more affluent people he knew who he wanted to help. He found them a little intimidating. So I suggested he try the wording, which, as it turned out, worked really well.

After church one day, Ken went up to a highly accomplished acquaintance and said: "I know we've known each other for years, and I think you know that I'm a financial advisor, but it would be crazy of me not to mention that I specialize in helping executives such as yourself in making sure they're doing all the right things financially. I really believe it would be a good use of your time if we were to get together for lunch some time." The man agreed, and he has since become a great client.

And just today a client of mine in Louisiana called Cliff told me that this "silly" wording "breaks my barriers to asking."

The reason it is silly is because you are fairly sure you can help this person.

That's what should make it easy to bring up in conversation. It is about believing in yourself and what you do for a living and following the imperative that most of the time we need to ask for what we want.

John, a client of mine in Dallas, was sitting among other parents at his daughter's volleyball game. He found himself sitting near a parent who was reading a periodical on pensions and thought she could open a great business door. So he turned to her and said, "*Stacey, it's silly not to ask:* who would be the person to contact at your company about defined contribution (retirement) programs?" He went on to explain how his firm had cutting-edge research on the topic and helped companies like Stacey's all the time. Her response? "That would be me." This is a $500 million investment opportunity, and John now has an appointment.

Three weeks later I talked to John again. This time he told me that he'd just presented to an association of high-end lawyers in a five-state region. Afterward he had approached the national president and said, "It would be silly of me not to suggest that I think we should be doing this presentation to all the states." Now he has a meeting at the national headquarters to get this ball rolling.

Recruiting? "*It would be silly of me* not to mention that I might be able to help you professionally. My company is always looking out for high-caliber individuals who enjoy working with people and want to make a difference in the world. We work in the ABC industry, and I'd be happy to chat more with you and see if it might be a good fit."

Selling a product that helps fill a need? "Based on what you were saying about X, *it would be silly of me* not to mention that my company helps people in this situation, or with this problem."

As with all ideas, play with the wording until it sounds like something you would say. Also, try it more than once. There's no magic pill.

You might prefer similar wording: "It would be remiss of me not to mention ...," "It would make no sense for me not to mention ...," "It would be mad or daft or ridiculous or foolish [find your thesaurus!] if I didn't mention..."

USE AN AGENDA

What's the number one excuse people use for not asking for referrals? *"I always forget to ask."*

Most of the time, what they *really mean* is *"I am not comfortable asking."*

Getting comfortable asking is the most important piece in developing a thriving referral business. That's what Chapters 1 to 4 address.

Using a written agenda for meetings provides one solution to those who are comfortable asking for referrals or who are at least getting more comfortable. Although, come to think if it, even if you are not asking for referrals, your business will benefit. I promise.

Having a formal agenda may sound pretty trivial; but for many of you reading this, it is not.

There are many reasons to have a written agenda. Few top sales professionals are naturally organized, and few have the time to want to spend on creating agendas. But I believe it is another tool that will help you get more referrals.

You'll find a sample skeleton agenda and script later on in this chapter.

THE ADVANTAGES OF USING AN AGENDA

What are the advantages of using an agenda?

1. From a referral standpoint, the intent here is to plant the seed that there is more to the meeting than just what may be obvious (see the sample agenda that follows) and that there will be some kind of conversation around what your client is getting out of working with you that you can use to segue into having a referral conversation—provided your client is happy.

2. Using an agenda will help to make sure you commit to getting some positive feedback and not forget again or run the meeting too long.

3. It will help you see that getting great feedback allows a natural transition to a referral conversation.

4. It sets a different tone. Try using an agenda at least for a period of time. I have never heard any of my clients say they regretted using one. It will not *transform* your meetings, but many people say it sets a more professional tone. It may seem a bit stuffy to a few of you, but most people like dealing with organized professionals. No clients fully respect or prefer paying someone who flies by the seat of his pants on a regular basis—even though you may think it is fun. An agenda respects their time more and allows for a discussion of other priorities that may have changed since your last correspondence.

5. Your clients will appreciate it, even if they do so only subconsciously, because they like to know what to expect. They will feel more comfortable. Remember, certainty is a fundamental human need.

6. It will help you confront your real fears behind asking for referrals and help you start asking more effectively.

Here are a few tips about agendas:

1. **Make your agenda simple and very easy to duplicate** or **delegate it to someone else.** If you're conversing with me in your mind, saying, "Matt, this doesn't fit with my personality," reread the advantages, see if you really have these covered already, and keep reading.

2. **Give your client a copy of the agenda, preferably one that's exactly the same as yours.** This way it looks like you are both literally on the same page and you're not hiding anything.

   Note: If you are still perfecting your referral conversation and need written reminders for yourself (and you think you need to put them on your version of the agenda), try to keep them as brief and simple as possible and remove them as soon as you remember.

3. **Consider e-mailing or mailing your agenda out ahead of time.** This looks very professional and organized and, most important, gives your client a chance to make sure you are both in agreement about what will be discussed; as well, it avoids the kind of surprise that occurs when he or she walks in the door with a topic you're not prepared for.

4. **With prospects, have a conversation at the start of your meeting about how that person heard about you.** Regardless of what they say, it gives you a chance to say something like, "That's interesting! Pretty much everyone I work with these days was referred to me by someone else." Or "Most of my business comes from people saying nice things about me to other people." You are planting some seeds here. If most of your business comes from personal recommendations, that makes a statement to them about how well you run your business and about how others have felt strongly enough to put their integrity on the line to refer people to you.

5. **Focus on the client.** The wording and items in general on your agenda should focus on the client, not you.

6. **Don't use the word referrals** or **recommendations.** Put "feedback," or "mini survey," or "check-in," on your agenda. Do *not* use the word *referrals* on your agenda. This word is *dead*; it does not resonate positively with the general public anymore. It's been done to death and reminds people of signs they've seen at a grocery store bank or on too many business cards or e-mail signatures of salespeople. It's like the word *used*; used cars (formerly "secondhand" cars) became preowned cars and more recently are being called predriven cars. Next they will be called pretouched or pre-sat-down-in ... You get the point. Since you cannot have a referral conversation and ask for referrals unless you have earned them, first you need to verify that, indeed, you have earned them. The best way to do this is to have a conversation about what the biggest benefits have been to your client (see Step 2 in Chapter 6).

    Therefore, call your referral conversation something like "feedback," "value check-in," or perhaps "mini survey." Some salespeople I know have put on their agendas "helping others" or "other ways we help people you care about." All these can be effective *provided you are comfortable with them.*

    I am not an advocate for calling it anything more obvious (such as "introductions" or "personal recommendations" or anything tacky that more or less says "help me grow my business." This is partly because today's consumer is more aware of older-school sales techniques and because those techniques scream the "me, me, me" approach. It turns people off.

7. **Use your time wisely.** You'll notice that getting positive feedback does not come last on the agenda. You don't want to run out of time. Again, the healthiest mindset is that the discussion is not intended to benefit you (it will, but your client doesn't care about

that); it's to help people that your client cares about. In other words, recommending you is a value-added service. For example, it's like the time you recommended a friend to your chiropractor and your friend returned from her appointment delighted because of how much better her back felt. How did you feel after that?

8. Item 7 on the sample agenda that follows is intended as the assumed close—that you expect the client to do business with you. You can still reduce the prospect's resistance by saying, "If you think this looks like a good fit for you, then we'll schedule our next appointment. If you don't think this is best for you, we won't; but hopefully you'll at least have learned something beneficial. How does that sound?"

But you still have *your* expectation firmly in black and white on the agenda.

9. Last, a client of mine, Rich, taught me that if you don't like the word *agenda*, call it a *discussion outline*.

SAMPLE AGENDA FOR INITIAL MEETING

The agenda for the initial meeting would likely look a lot like this:

Name:_____Date: _____

How did you hear about me?

1. Tell me about you. Update your info. Your expectations.

2. (*optional*) Why me or why ABC Company *or* About me or About my expectations.

3. Your objectives for today's meeting:

   a.

   b.

   c.

4. Other ways I can help you: (list).

5. Feedback.

6. Q&A.

7. Schedule next appointment or annual review.

Sample Agenda Script

The following sets a friendly tone and a firm direction for the meeting:

Before we get started, I'd just like to go over the agenda quickly. Oh, and do you still have till 3 p.m.? Great. Well, first off, I want to make sure we have all your contact information up to date, and I would like to know a little bit about you and find out what your expectations are of me. Then the primary reason for our meeting today is to take a look at your [for example] investment goals and see if there are any better ways that suit your needs than what you are already doing. After that I'd like to quickly go over a few other ways I can help you, get a little feedback to make sure this was a good use of your time, answer any remaining questions you have, and then, if everything looks good to us, schedule your next appointment. How does that sound?

DO IT!

Make up a simple generic agenda that you can start using, print 50 copies of it, and see how it helps to set a calmer, more professional tone at your meetings.

HAVE AN EXPECTATIONS DISCUSSION

Do you know everything your clients expect from you? Do *they* know everything *you* expect from them? Consider having an expectations discussion to express your value, minimize miscommunication, and increase referrals. Here's how.

Several years ago I was having lunch with a CPA friend of mine who was casually explaining to me that he told all his prospective clients that he expected them to send him business if they were going to work together. *Really?* I had heard this from many top producers before. Finally the lightbulb went on in my head. Why can't we all do this?

Perhaps we can. The road to getting there is to have a two-part "expectations discussion" in which, provided that you meet their expectations, clients will refer new prospects to you. If you already have a lot of existing clients, integrating this into your conversations is no problem: it's never too late to revisit how you are doing. But you can also take this approach up front with new prospects, and the feedback you get can even help you with client retention.

WHY EXPECTATIONS MATTER

Don't you feel better when you know what to expect? Generally speaking, people like certainty. When you fly somewhere, the pilot tells you how long the flight is, which route you'll be taking, what altitude you'll be flying at, what the movie is, etc. If only my dentist would do the same. Whenever I go, he doesn't explain what he's going to do or how long anything is going to take. When the drilling starts, all I can do is white-knuckle my hands, think about lying on a beach somewhere, try to recall how many fillings I'm scheduled to have, and pray the agony will be over soon; it is *awful*. Don't put your clients through this!

Beginning the Conversation

Here's my solution: *really impress your clients with everything you bring to the table.* Set yourself apart by being exceptionally professional and making them feel very comfortable. We all like to know what to expect. Below is part one of a sample conversation that allows you to find out your client's expectations of you. Keep in mind this is a sample version that you would want to personalize:

You: Before we really get into our meeting today, I'd like to find out a little bit more about what your expectations are from us potentially working together. What are you looking for in a good financial advisor?

(I think it is better to pause here and let the client respond because he or she will not be able to think of much.)

You: Thanks. That's all good to know. I've put together a list of some things that other clients have said they expect from me. I'm curious: what else on this list is something you consider to be important?

Have the prospect look over the list and identify other things that matter to him or her:

1. Have integrity and work in *your* best interest.

2. Care about you, your assets, and your financial security.

3. Look out for you, bring a sense of control to your financial situation, and help create more confidence about the future.

4. Ask questions and listen well to truly understand your needs and goals.

5. Consistently provide high-quality service regardless of how much you invest.

6. Bring more balance to your financial life and help you do the things you need to do for your future (whether you feel like it or not!).

7. Provide my financial expertise and experience and stay current on changes in the investment world that you don't have the time to do.

8. Put in the time that you probably don't have to devote to your accounts, or portfolio, or policies.

9. Buy you lunch once every year.

10. Be your financial coach.

11. Give you 100 percent of my best effort.

12. Help you reduce your taxes, if possible.

13. Help you with other insurance and investment needs.

14. Meet with you at least quarterly or annually for financial reviews.

15. Probably not be in a very good mood if [insert the name of your favorite team] lost last weekend!

16. Return your phone calls as soon as possible (always within 24 hours).

17. Utilize all my resources (including my assistant or team) to best handle your concerns, questions, and requests.

18. Advocate for your business.

19. Make sure your investments fit with your own principles, values, and risk tolerance.

20. Serve as your financial advisor for the long term.

You: Can you think of anything else that's really important to you?

You: How does this sound?

The Key Ingredients—and Why They Work

Clearly you need to personalize the list to fit your business, your niche, and even your sense of humor. One financial advisor included

"Provide unbiased advice even though I'm a Dallas Cowboys fan." A Realtor I know put "Bring farm-fresh eggs every once in a while." I think it's important to have a little humor in it, for one thing, so you don't come across as too heavy and, for another, so the prospect will think, "She's got a good sense of humor; she seems pretty nice." Here's why this approach works.

You Can Counter Objections

One other thing that makes this a clever approach is that you can include in your list a counter to every objection you've ever heard from people who didn't work with you. In other words, close people on whatever concerns they might have but might not verbalize. Prospects think you look rather young? Tell them your clients expect fresh, innovative ideas backed by a company with reputable expertise. Tell them your clients expect enthusiasm and stellar client service that is above and beyond what they could normally expect from a veteran in your industry. Tell them you specialize in serving the needs of clients in their industry and have more experience than many veterans in working with people in their profession. Find what clients may perceive is your weakness and make it your strength.

You Set Yourself Apart

More than anything else, you will really set yourself apart by having this conversation. If you don't believe me, you should try being on the receiving end of an expectations discussion.

It's important to allow prospects time to think of their own concerns and to give them time to talk about the list and what they like about it.

My personal favorite is number 18. Can you imagine going to a bank to open an account and hearing, "Sarah, I'm fortunate enough to know a lot of people in this community. Another thing you can expect from me—once I know a little bit more about you and your business—is that I would be happy to introduce you to some people who might want to do business with you." You're hearing about ways to make money for your business and saying to yourself, "I thought I was here to get sold something!"

YOU SET UP AN "EMOTIONAL BANK ACCOUNT"

Based on author Stephen Covey's "emotional bank account" concept, this conversation lays out expectations and begins the relationship on solid ground. The premise of the emotional bank account is that without you clearly explaining what value you bring from the start, personality clashes and communication breakdowns can result. People judge us based on their expectations of us, and most of the time these are only implicit and have not been discussed.

PART TWO OF THE CONVERSATION: YOUR EXPECTATIONS

Now that you've clarified what the prospects expect from you and you've impressed them with all that you bring to the table, it's your turn to lay out your expectations. Once again, you will want to tweak the wording to fit your personality, your job, and the words you would use:

You: Great! Well, now that I'm clear on what matters to you, there are a *few* things that I ask for in return.

You: I ask … (*read the list out loud*):

1. That you laugh at my jokes

2. That you arrive within 10 minutes of all scheduled meetings or call to say that you will be late

3. That you return my calls within 24 to 48 hours

4. That you come prepared with all necessary documentation

5. That provided that I meet all your expectations, you will think about people important to you in your life (whether that's at work or in your family) and consider recommending that they at least have a conversation with me to make sure they have all their ducks in a row

6. That you let me know of any significant changes in your life or changes in your goals

7. That you mostly follow my recommendations

8. That you at least fake an interest in fishing if I start talking about it

You: Does that sound fair enough?

What I love about this part of the discussion is that you're no longer a needy salesperson. You're confidently asserting that you have expectations for a healthy working relationship. I'd suggest that your list be much shorter than what the prospect can expect from you and that you start out with a couple of very light requests. This portion of the conversation allows you to:

Plant the seeds for future referrals whenever value is provided. The real intent of this part of the conversation is point 5 in the expectations list above. Once you've stated it, it gives you permission to return to it any time whether it's the next day, week, month, or year. "Michelle, do you remember the discussion we had the first time we met? How am I doing? (*Or:* Am I doing what I said I would do for you?)"

Once you've verified that you are indeed doing a great job, you can go on to say, "I don't know if you remember this, but one of the things I asked from you was that if I was meeting your expectations, in return you would think of people you care about and suggest that they have a quick conversation with me to make sure they have all their ducks in a row."

Determine that you are living up to your prospect's expectations. By the way, if for some reason you don't hear great things, move to plan B. Rather than ask for referrals, simply ask how you need to improve and then address it immediately. That's how raving fans are won.

Once you have consent for referrals, use Steps 3 to 6 in the Six-Step Fearless Referral Conversation in Chapter 6.

Get confirmation that your expectations are reasonable. After you've covered point 5 from your expectations list, continue on without a pause to points 6 and 7. Remember to finish by getting the prospect's consent that your expectations are reasonable.

DO IT!

Have an expectations discussion that fits your business and your niche. It will go a long way toward building trust and will position you as an up-front professional who isn't afraid to have tough discussions. These discussions prevent misunderstandings and give you a way to communicate your experience and the value you provide clients.

CHAPTER 6

THE SIX STEPS TO A FEARLESS REFERRAL CONVERSATION

Before I started Matt's referral coaching, I was asking by saying, "I build my business by referral; do you know of anyone I could help?"

I would often get a "Let me think about that." I also would get referrals that never materialized into meetings. With Matt's help, I have a method to get consistent referrals that are turning into business. In the past five months, I've generated over 40 new referrals, opened 10 new clients, and have in excess of 100 million dollars in my newly built pipeline.

—Stephen Lewis, Principal, Bernstein Global
Wealth Management

FOLLOW THE SIX STEPS TO A FEARLESS REFERRAL CONVERSATION

These six steps are ones that I have tested over the years and that my clients find to be the most effective way to get high-quality referrals on a consistent basis.

The good news is that the steps are easy to understand. However, it does take some practice to implement them and get results. You should also note that while all the steps are included for a reason, you don't have to use all of them. The ones you must use pretty much every time are Steps 3, 5, and 6. But to start with, get familiar with all of them because they will help you.

I am reminded of a time I was traveling in the Netherlands and I learned enough Dutch to walk into a McDonald's and order a sundae (I guess small things impressed me when I was 20!). So I knew enough to get what I wanted. The only problem was that I didn't understand anything else I was asked! Did I want nuts on the sundae? Was my order for here or to go? Nor would I have understood the amount I owed except by then the woman behind the counter was speaking English to me. The six-step referral conversation is the same way. Using a bit of it will help but will not get you all you need.

My advice is this: implement Steps 1 and 2 right away. As you feel comfortable and competent with them, add another step at a time.

Here are the six steps in brief:

Step 1. Acknowledge your client. This is your opportunity to powerfully commend your client. Acknowledgment (recognition) is the primary human need we have after food, clothing, and shelter. It sets the right tone for a potential referral request.

Step 2. Get positive feedback. "What has been most valuable about the work we've done so far?" Have you helped your client reach a personal goal? Put your client on the path to financial security? Having a conversation around the value that your client has received helps you determine if you have earned the referral. You only ask if you have.

Step 3. Get specific. It is your job to help the client identify a few specific people who might be open to hearing from you. This is the most important step, and it's not one that comes easily. Most people who ask lose the opportunity for a referral by saying, "If you know any other people I should talk to, please have them give me a call." You need to be much more specific.

Step 4. Reassure your client. Reassuring your client gets worked into the conversation in the wording of Step 3. Your clients often need to hear from you that they are not expected to know the needs of their friends or associates. It helps reduce their resistance and apprehension.

Step 5. Coach your client on what to say. It is your job to make sure the referral source has something simple and effective to say to the person he or she is referring. Most people do not know how to introduce you, and this way the referral opportunity is not lost because they either say the wrong thing or (more likely) get cold feet and say nothing.

Step 6. Keep control of the process. You cannot simply hope your contact information will be passed on, so that you can just sit by the phone and wait for it to ring. You need to make sure you always have control of the next step. You need to follow up with your client first to see if the referral has been "warmed up" and wants to talk to you. Getting this permission increases the client's responsibility to following through and avoids issues with "do not call."

USE STEP 1: ACKNOWLEDGE YOUR CLIENT

Based on all the research and every study ever done of what it takes to be successful and fulfilled in our society, exceptional people—like you and those in our network—are either in the top 10 percent of their industry or moving that way. How do I know this? Because only people such as yourselves—the elite top 10 percent—take the time to read sales litera-ture like this and develop themselves professionally and personally. This isn't just some clichéd sales advice: read almost any autobiography of a top performer, from Serena Williams to Brian Tracy to Stephen King. They are students of their field, *and* they take action on what they learn. You already have one of the most challenging jobs in our society dealing with rejection and setbacks daily, so through your persistence, learning, and action, you put yourself in the top 10 percent, if not this year, then in the next three to seven years.

There. That's me acknowledging you, and I mean every word of it.

The purpose of Step 1 is to make your clients feel good. You do this by commending your clients for the smart decisions they have made.

People love it.

Even if they have made some poor choices in the past, they will appreciate you highlighting what they got right.

Taking time to acknowledge others is *powerful*. I learned this idea from a sales manager named Dutch. If there is a secret weapon to improving relationships quickly, this is it. Robert Cialdini might call it complimenting people, but rather than saying "My, what brown eyes you've got," the goal is to be factual about identifying a trait or action that has produced positive results.

In 1896 it was Thomas Edison talking to Henry Ford (who was his next-door neighbor). Ford was explaining how he was develop-ing a gasoline car. Edison thumped the table and not only exclaimed that it was a great idea but also explained why he felt that way. Ford was later to write, "That bang on the table was worth worlds to me. No man up to then had given me any encouragement …, here, all at once, and out of a clear sky, the greatest inventive genius in the world had given me complete approval."

Today things are no different. People are crying out for positive recognition. This is why recent best-selling authors, such as Tim Sanders and Keith Ferrazzi, are such strong advocates for open, authentic, and meaningful relationships in the workplace. Proof of this is demonstrated in Tom Rath and Donald Clifton's *How Full Is Your Bucket?* They cite Gallup research that found two things: (1) lack of recognition is the main reason why Americans leave their jobs, and (2) 65 percent of Americans received no recognition in the workplace in 2003. Lack of income actually came in fifth place. Once you start getting good at this, you will be surprised by how much others appreciate your feedback.

This is not some fake exercise about glossing over something unsightly. People will see through that. But when you put some thought into what your client has done that many other people haven't, your recognition will be received with sincere gratitude. After all, if 50,000 thoughts go through our heads each day, and on average 80 percent of them are negative, we can be assured that most people spend much of their time berating themselves.

There are three rules to your acknowledgment:

1. It must be sincere.
2. It must be specific.
3. It must be true.

This is not as easy as it may sound. There's a reason why few people do this and do it well. For those of you who are naturally empathic, you probably already do this. But you are in a small minority. For most of us, it takes practice—quite a lot of practice. I have found this a difficult skill to master.

If 10 of us were to put this book down right now and go and coach soccer for a group of 12-year-olds, the "feedback" that about

8 of us would give them at the end of the practice would likely be something general such as "Good job guys—well played." It's the business equivalent of "Thanks for coming in today; it was nice to see you." This is empty, white-bread content that provides no useful feedback.

But to take the time to think of specific actions and character traits demonstrated is altogether different—and the other person knows it too. What specific things has this person done that merit recognition above what every other person does in a similar situation? *In other words: what does this person do that most would consider above and beyond?*

♦ What qualities did this person need to make the specific wise choices that he or she did?

♦ In other words, can you acknowledge the person for courage or persistence?

♦ Where did the person show self-discipline or sacrifice instead of making an easier choice?

♦ Where did the person take a higher level of responsibility compared with what others did?

People go to greater lengths and take creditable actions with one of their passions—is it with their children? Their pet? A hobby? A service project? Can this relate to your line of work or conversations you might have with the person you are acknowledging? Even my hairdresser, Brittany, pointed out to me that not many people would spend five hours on a Saturday to work on their book. That made me feel acknowledged.

Matt Loverine, one of my recent clients, is so effective at Step 1 that he will often be given referrals on the spot. He makes people feel so good about themselves for the wise decisions they have made, that their brain instantly starts to think of others who would like to feel the same way. "You should talk to the other guys in my department," a client will say, or "You know, my sister should meet with you." I cannot tell you this happens often for other people, but I do believe that much of that is because most people are really weak at the skill of acknowledging others.

I remember Matt sharing with me one example in which he was working with a client who had just been downsized from a car plant after 30 years. This man had saved his money over the years, and Matt shared with him his utter disbelief that some of this autoworker's peers had done the same and yet decided to spend their savings rather than reinvest them. As he slapped his own knee to emphasize how crazy he thought this was, he said, "I met with two of your coworkers. One of them blew all his money on a Harley after he was let go, and the other decided to spend 22 years of his carefully set-aside savings and blow it all on a trip to Vegas! Believe me: you will be so happy with yourself five years from now—and as you hit 70 and 80 years old."

Ideally, strive to make the other person feel as though he or she is in a small minority of the population who makes wise decisions.

If you have third-party statistics, I would recommend using one or two because then you won't sound biased or as if you are making something up.

EXAMPLE 1

You might say:

> *Before we wrap up, I want to take a moment to commend you for deciding to take proactive steps about your retirement future today. I'm sure there were more fun things you could have done with this time, but that's why successful people are willing to do the things unsuccessful people are not, even though successful people don't feel like doing those things either!*

Amazingly, 55 percent of Americans with retirement plans are receiving no professional guidance. They are walking around blind. Kudos to you for taking the bull by the horns and getting yourself out of a potentially perilous situation. Ignorance is not always bliss.

EXAMPLE 2

This next example makes general reference to the three areas the client has made decisions on—which can be an effective strategy.

Before we talk about next steps here, I want to acknowledge you for taking the action you have. Procrastinating on the decisions we have made about your estate, your legacy, and how you want to invest in the next five years would have been easy to do. It's easy to ignore something like long-term planning when you're as busy as I know you are, but this is precisely the kind of planning that too many people ignore and then regret later in life.

I came across a fairly recent article the other day, in a 2004 Journal of Political Economy, *which reported that the average American—58 percent—spends more time picking out a new tennis racket or TV set than deciding on a contribution rate and investment allocation on a retirement plan. So I hope you realize how wise this time investment has been!*

DO IT!

Everybody likes recognition. You've likely heard the expression "Feedback is the breakfast of champions." I first read it in Spencer Johnson's The One Minute Manager. *This is your opportunity to say positive things to your client for making some good decisions.*

At your next opportunity, think ahead of time, "What could I genuinely commend this person for? What has always impressed me about this person?"

Recently a client of mine, Bill, reported that twice in the previous two weeks he had complimented different lawyers for how they build relationships with their clients, rather than just treating them as transactions. He did it so well that each of them said to him on the spot, "Actually, Bill, there's a client of mine I'd like you to meet. I think you could help him."

Once you are talking to people who are feeling very good about themselves, it now becomes your turn to ask for positive feedback. This is very important!

USE STEP 2: GET POSITIVE FEEDBACK

The purpose of Step 2 is to find out whether you have earned the right to ask for a referral. What value have your clients received? You will hear in the tone of their voices how pleased they are and whether you can ask for a referral (or not).

The focus here is to get *positive* feedback that builds on the feel-good factor of Step 1. People refer you when they are most happy with the work you have done. I first read about this idea from the referral training veteran Bill Cates. The point of this question is to hear whether you have a green light to ask about referrals. *Remember, the six steps are a train of thought*—not something contrived. You only ask for referrals if the client is happy.

You are not asking for feedback in general. Get that some other time! If the person is not that thrilled with what you have done, you will hear qualification in the person's voice when you ask—so you don't need to worry that this is an artificial exercise. If there is something you sense the person is concerned about, go ahead and find out what it is, because asking for referrals at that point would be a mistake.

To get positive feedback, ask, "I'm always curious to find out: what has been most valuable about the work that we have done so far?"

And when you do, keep these three things in mind:

♦ **Be silent and let the person talk.**

♦ **Dig!** Feel free to ask, "Anything else besides that?" after the client responds. The more value the client can verbalize, the better. One reason this is important is because many people need time to think hard to give you the highest-quality answer. The first words that come out of their mouths might not be the most meaningful.

♦ **Also ask, "What value did you receive that you did not expect?** This is a wonderful question that I learned from an excellent personal coach I worked with called Simon Reilly. Not everyone will have a response, but those who do may surprise you with terrific feedback you would not otherwise get. Steve, one of my recent clients, said to me, "Matt, I find I'm enjoying my job a lot more."

What are the most important things in this conversation?

♦ You want to get your clients *talking about how they feel.*

♦ Don't be afraid to ask in addition, "How do you feel about what we've done?"

♦ The ultimate feeling is peace of mind—even if they don't use those exact words. We are more giving when we feel good, and we want them to give more referrals!

♦ For some of my clients, Step 2 is the game changer. It can feel really good to get this feedback, and it makes the asking easier! This should give you the green light to ask for referrals. Even if you know the client is already happy, the feedback you get can still be valuable and may teach you what your clients consider most useful compared with your own opinion.

Some other ideas about this conversation:

♦ **Feel free to reword the question slightly.** If you prefer the words *helpful, useful, important,* use them. You could even ask, "What has been the best takeaway for you from our meeting today, or from the work we've done together over the past four years?" or "What have you gotten most out of our meetings so far?"

♦ **The question *must* be open-ended.** Don't say, "Was the meeting helpful? Good. Now, who else should I speak with?" One reason for this is that most people are polite and will simply nod their heads to avoid appearing rude or to avoid a potential confrontation. It will not give you an accurate response.

♦ **Avoid asking, "How am I doing?"** People do not know how to respond to a question such as this. They say, "Fine." Nobody is going to go to bat for you and recommend you to others based on just feeling "fine"!

♦ **Write down what your clients say for feedback.** Using their words when making your referral request will be much more impactful than saying something generic like "Who else might benefit from talking to me?"

♦ **Take notes.** If your client seems a little unsure what to say, it pays to take notes during your meetings and make a mental note of instances where you believe you brought value, education, and ideas, because many of us will forget—especially if the relationship has been going on for a while. In fact, most people have a terrible memory for where they were when they started with you, and we do have a tendency to fool ourselves into thinking that we made most of the progress on our own. Remind them in a super nice way of the reality!

♦ **Provided you get a really positive response, you have earned the right to have a referral conversation. If it's less than very positive, you should not attempt to ask for referrals.** You can't quick-fix relationships. Don't waste your time or your client's and push the relationship in the wrong direction. Instead, find out how you can better serve this person and then address the concern; most likely your client will then become a raving fan because you actually cared enough to listen and respond. There's a reason every success story ever written includes the message "Press on. Nothing in the world can take the place of persistence."

Finally, here are two examples of conversations.

EXAMPLE 1

You: I'm always curious to find out: What has been most valuable for you about the work that we've done together?

Client: I like the fact you're easy to work with; you're relaxed. Well, and I trust your advice. You know your stuff.

You: Thank you! Anything else besides that?

Client: It's nice not to have to worry about this stuff. And you always get back to us quickly. I like that. And I feel like I can call you any time—that's nice, especially since I don't think much about finances except on the weekends.

(Now you've got positive feedback, the green light is on, and it's time to transition to Step 3. Remember, you don't have to ask in the very next sentence. You could end the meeting right now and wait until you are packing up or on your way out—so long as you have enough time.)

You: I appreciate that; I know it's important. Last time we met, you mentioned Gabe, your brother-in-law in Colorado, and noted that he wasn't too happy with his current advisor. How would you recommend finding out if he might be open to connecting with me at some point?

EXAMPLE 2

Consultant: I'm always curious to find out: What has been most important for you about the work that we've done together?

Client: It's been very helpful. I'm glad to have a plan in place for my family and know they'll be taken care of—whatever happens.

Consultant: I'm glad to hear that. Anything else besides that?

Client: Well, I think you do a good job of explaining everything. I've had experiences in the past where the person I was meeting with would—well, I'd just get confused—and I felt awkward admitting I didn't really understand what he was saying.

Consultant: Yes, I try not to bamboozle people!

Client: And I'd also have to say that you asked me some really important questions that I had not considered, so I think what we came up with is very strong.

Consultant: How do you feel about that?

Client: A lot better!

(Again, as noted in Example 1, now that you've received positive feedback, the green light is on, and it's time to transition to Step 3. Remember, you don't have to ask in the very next sentence. You could end the meeting right now and wait until you are packing up or on your way out—so long as you have enough time.)

Consultant: I'm happy to hear that. You know, I'd really like to meet your business partner, Al. I don't know if the two of you talk about this kind of planning much, but he sounds like a great guy, and it's very rare that I meet someone in his situation that I can't help. What would be the best way to find out if he might be open to hearing from me sometime?

Do you always need to get positive feedback? I don't think so. There are times when your intuition is strong enough that you just know that your client is really pleased with your work. Often there may be dead giveaway things they say, and sometimes there may be more subtle exclamations such as "Really? I didn't know that" or "That's really helpful." If in any doubt, you've nothing to lose by finding out how you've made a difference.

DO IT!

So when should you do it? At your very next meeting. This is the easiest step to start doing right away!

USE STEP 3: WHY YOU MUST GET SPECIFIC

The purpose of Step 3 is for you to identify whom you would like your client to introduce you to (it's not the client's job to figure it out).

Most of the time by "specific," I mean that you are asking about one to three actual people who easily come to your client's mind.

Step 3 is the most important step of all. You can do everything right and get no referrals because you are being too vague about whom you would like to help.

DON'T BE AFRAID

First you need to understand why you are afraid to get specific. The so-called logic is that lots of people would benefit from meeting you (I don't doubt that this is true!) and that if you keep it nice and general, you cast a wide net and increase your chances of there being a few fish at the end of the day.

Unfortunately the shotgun approach backfires on the human brain, which needs focus and simplicity to identify a target for you. It's one reason why there are no referrals for people who tell others they can help "any small- to medium-size business" or that "if you know any people looking to buy or sell in the next six months, have them give me a call." Nothing sticks in the mind. There is nothing for the brain to focus on.

WHY IT MATTERS

There are two reasons to get so specific that the person you are talking to narrows down options in his or her brain to two or three people.

REASON 1. THE AVERAGE PERSON KNOWS TOO MANY PEOPLE

On average, people know 200 to 250, whether they realize it or not, and they need your help to think of someone specific. Well, who comes to your mind when I ask you these questions?

- Do you know anyone who might benefit from my services?
- Do you know anyone who likes sports?
- Do you know anyone who likes to grill out in the summertime?

◆ Do you know any business owners I could help?

◆ Do you know anyone that would like to reduce stress by getting more referrals?

◆ Do you know anyone who would like to make more money by getting more referrals?

So are you tripping over names left and right and scrambling to write them down and send them to me?

Or were you overwhelmed by a fog because so many people fit that bill that you've no idea where to start?

Your clients are exactly the same. *You've got to make it easy for them!*

REASON 2. EVERYBODY IS CRAZY BUSY

They are not going to talk to eight different people for you because they don't have time. If they don't leave the meeting with someone in mind, very few of them are going to spend any more time trying to think of "anyone."

I can't emphasize this enough: *Step 3 is the most important step of all.*

Never again say, "If you can think of anyone who can benefit from my services, please have the person give me a call." When you use the word *anyone*, they will think of no one.

And "Do you know anyone else I should be talking to in a similar situation to yours?" isn't much better. It's almost always too vague. Get specific!

ASK DIRECTLY FOR A SPECIFIC PERSON

Once again, the purpose of Step 3 is for you to identify specifically whom you would like your client to introduce you to (it is not your client's job to identify anyone!).

So what are the best ways to get specific? There are two effective ways to transition immediately from Step 2, getting positive feedback. One is to ask directly about a specific person, and the other is to ask the expert, your client, for his or her advice.

As soon as the other person is done giving you great feedback and it is clear the person has recognized good value, you say, "Thanks for that [feedback]," and you move straight into your next train of thought—helping someone else:

Directly ask for the person you want to meet. Make sure it is someone your client likes!

EXAMPLE

Here's one example of how you might approach things: "In the past you've mentioned that you know Megan Gibbs pretty well. Now, I don't know if the two of you ever talk about the type of work we've done together [Step 4], but *I would really appreciate you introducing us.*"

Alternative versions could be "*I'd love to meet her. Is there any chance you could set up a lunch for the three of us some time?*" or "*I think I could really help her in similar ways that we've worked together. Do you think she might be open to meeting with me?*"

Now, it is hoped you've been doing your fishing and preplanning your asks because this will make Step 3 so much easier, and it will make you feel much more confident. Here are five other ways to help you get more specific.

LISTEN FOR AND WRITE DOWN SPECIFIC
INDIVIDUALS YOUR CLIENTS MENTION

Reread the section in Chapter 4 on fishing for referrals. Write down names that come up because clearly you want to find the right time to bring them up again.

Doing this sounds so simple and obvious, but what I've found is that *it is not obvious to everyone*. Many salespeople are so focused on what they are explaining that *they are not listening* for what some could mistakenly consider to be irrelevant asides.

I used to think everyone listened, but one day I was making this observation to an insurance agent and he gave me a completely blank look. In his mind, if he was explaining homeowner's policy coverage options to a customer, he was doing it 100 percent. He did not have 10 percent of his radar out should the customer mention other people = potential business opportunities.

Now when I mention this to audiences, *everyone* gives me a blank look because those who do it think everyone does it and those who don't do it have no idea what I'm talking about!

EDUCATE YOUR CLIENTS

It's up to you to educate your clients on what a qualified referral is. Seek out a clear *similarity* that will narrow down the choice to one to three people.

The transition statement from Step 2 is:

♦ "Thanks! It's interesting: what I find is that the people I can help the most are …"

Or:

♦ "I've been working lately with a lot of people like you who are …"

Or:

♦ "I've really been specializing lately on working with other people who are …"

Here are some other scenarios:

- **Same life situation as yours.** Selling a business, just had a baby, just got downsized, very close to retirement, seeking a new job, just got married, families with special needs children, recently widowed

- **Same profession.** Other partners in the firm, architects, dairy farmers, also business owners of companies with more than X number of employees (likely in the same industry)

- **Same job title.** HR directors (even better, in the paper industry)

- **Same demographic.** Indian physicians, also residents of Sunny Pines neighborhood

- **Same religion.** Lutheran men 50–65, on the finance committee at church

- **Same employer.** Employees at Xerox

- **Same pastime.** Also curious about income properties

- **Same frustration or pain.** With the staff turnover at their current bank, with the service they're getting from their current cell phone provider, always having to go back for more chiropractic adjustments

- **Same life challenge.** Know they don't have the time or expertise to work on this

PRE-PREPARE A LIST OF PROSPECTS TO PRESENT TO YOUR POTENTIAL REFERRAL SOURCE

Overall, this approach works well if you are comfortable using it. I feel it is more natural to have sourced names through conversation, but I know that's not always possible for everyone, and I know using a list works because I've had plenty of clients who have had success with it.

The Internet can be a great source of information for finding connections. A company Web site might have a list of industries it serves or testimonials from happy clients—sometimes even a client list. Being connected on LinkedIn or other social networking sites can also be a way of seeing whom someone is connected to—although just because a person is on someone's page doesn't mean the relationship is strong. Be sensitive to that when you bring it up.

Eric Heiting runs a financial planning practice named Physician Wealth Strategies. His clients are almost all doctors and are so busy that they are rarely going to make the time to call referrals and recommend him. He has great success showing them a list of references of doctors who have given him permission to use their names and then shows the new client a list of other physicians in their department. Next he asks a specific question, "Is there anyone here from your department who started quite recently?" Or he might ask, "Who else from your department has a stay-at-home spouse?" Or "Who else from your department has children in high school?"

Pat Marget is managing director of Executive Benefits Network, a company that specializes in working with banks. He has had success by first presenting to his current client a list of other banks that are in the same state and then saying to that bank president, "I'd really like to be able to help others in the same way. From this list, where else do you have good connections where you might be comfortable putting in a good word for me?"

Peggy David is the marketing director for her husband Jerry's business. He works mostly with business owners. Whenever he has an upcoming meeting with one of them where he knows he has brought good value (Step 2), she researches the Internet for similar businesses to the one owned by the person Jerry is about to meet. Then he has three separate questions. He begins by saying, "I do have another quick question for you":

◆ "How well do you know any of these people?"
◆ "Could you tell me a little bit about them?"

♦ "Now, I don't expect you to know how happy they are with their current advisor [Step 4], but would you be willing to introduce me to any of them?"

Then he uses Steps 5 and 6.

Chris Anderson used to specialize in helping teachers with their retirement planning and had similar success with that approach. Everyone has favorite coworkers, and there are always new staff members to help.

Be sensitive to the flip side. I have trained in companies where some of the salespeople were uncomfortable about being asked to talk to a client and produce a list of the client's neighbors! I don't blame them. And that shouldn't be necessary. A conversation can usually elicit who is important in that person's life.

The list is also helpful when there are a lot of people to choose from or to jog someone's memory: "These are a number of local companies I've identified as ones I can really help. Do you have any contacts at any of these?" I recommend this tactic highly if you're in a networking group that meets regularly.

USE GENERIC SPECIFICS

Use "generic" specifics such as *sibling, favorite coworker,* or *best friend* rather than *family, friends,* or *business associates* (too vague). Generic specifics help to narrow things down and work much better. Overly vague terms such as *friends, family members,* and *coworkers* are too much. Nobody is going to talk to 15 coworkers, but people might talk to 1 or 2. I urge you to try this.

HAVE A "NEW CAR" CONVERSATION

While this is more of a technique and not one I hear about much anymore, depending on your business you might find this idea useful.

161

"You know how when you buy a new car, you suddenly notice how everyone else seems to be driving the same car as you. It's rather like when ... [give an example such as being pregnant, being on crutches, etc.]. Well now that you're starting a family, or investing in income property, you probably seem to be talking to other people who are in the same situation ..."

There is no reason you should ever again hear, "I can't think of anyone."

If you are hearing this, go back and reread the section on fishing for referrals and the whole above segment. Your client isn't going to come up with names. If you want referrals, it's your job to do your homework.

OR ASK THE EXPERT!

I love this approach, and it works really well.

Remember, Step 3 is about working with your client to identify whom you can help next. That's it: who's next?

Ask the Expert means ask for the *advice* of the other person. Most people *love* to give advice.

EXAMPLE 1

Dr. Lee works at ABC Clinic, where one of his benefits is $400,000 in life insurance. His wife is a stay-at-home mother. According to Thomas J. Stanley's research in *Marketing to the Affluent*, 9 in 10 physicians do a very poor job managing their finances. Most doctors need closer to $2 million to $3 million to be properly covered. If Dr. Lee were to die prematurely, his wife would be in a really challenging situation.

My point here is that when you ask the "expert," you are safely assuming that there are many other people in the same situation in that client's affinity group that likely could use the help (usually a work department, team members, other partners in the firm, other nurses on the ward, other teachers in the same grade level, other board members, etc.).

You: Thanks for the feedback [transition from Step 2]. One of the things I'm curious about, Dr. Lee, is I can't imagine that you are the only physician in your department who only had the $400,000 of insurance coverage. Now I'm guessing you don't spend much time discussing different types of life insurance with your colleagues [Step 4], but *what would be the best way to find out if this is something that might be of value to the other physicians in your department?*

Then you close your mouth and wait expectantly for a helpful response.

EXAMPLE 2

Your software company has just had great feedback from a title company client.

You: That's great to hear. I'm delighted you're so pleased. You know, it would be fun to work with some other title companies on this kind of thing. I don't expect you would know the needs of other companies necessarily [Step 4], but *how would you recommend finding out who else might be interested in our software program?*

Here's why Ask the Expert works so well.

EVERYONE LIKES TO BE TREATED AS AN EXPERT AND GIVE ADVICE

Being treated like an expert makes your clients feel good, and you do not feel needy about asking! This is different from asking for help from a place of weakness. You are generating their suggestions. Let them think of the best way to get in touch with their referrals.

Eddy, a past client of mine from California, sought guidance from a minister client of his who was very pleased with the work Eddy had done.

"Minister, I was hoping you could give me some advice about how I might be able to help some of the more affluent members of your congregation in ways similar to how I've been able to help you."

The minister then went on to say that his church put on educational seminars every May and that Eddy should do some talks on financial topics. Eddy then asked him, "Who should I contact about setting these up?" to which he was told, "Call me."

Feeling emboldened, Eddy said, "Do you have any other suggestions for me?"

His client said, "Yes, we also own an assisted living facility by the church, and I think you should put on a workshop for the children of our residents."

THE FOCUS IS ON THEM

The focus is not about helping you; *it's about them helping others!* Remember, people refer you because it makes them feel good to help people they care about.

THE CLIENT TAKES RESPONSIBILITY AND OWNERSHIP OF THE PROCESS

That is powerful! *The client is committing to his or her idea rather than submitting to yours.* I would read that again.

This is not a sales conversation; it is a means to help other people by leveraging the expertise of your client, who will help if he or she knows, likes (Rule of Liking), and trusts you and has recognized your value (Rule of Reciprocation). And the power of the Rule of Commitment and Consistency (later in this chapter) works in your favor too.

THE QUESTION YOU ASK *Expects* A HELPFUL RESPONSE

Most of the time, your client will come up with something constructive, not least because you expect an intelligent response.

YOUR CLIENT MIGHT EXCEED EXPECTATIONS

By "asking the expert," you give your client the opportunity to suggest bigger and more creative opportunities than what you would have asked for.

Rather than just suggesting you call the other person, the client might recommend that you speak at an industry-related event or that he or she introduce you to that prospect personally—you never know!

Suzanne, a current client of mine in Chicago, wants to do more business in Kansas City. So she met with an insurance contact of hers and asked him how he'd suggest meeting some good estate planning attorneys.

He immediately produced a list of *all* the top attorneys in town, and not long after, Suzanne met with one who sat her by a wall that featured pictures of himself with the last three U.S. presidents! When Suzanne asked this attorney whom he would recommend for a particular type of client she sought, he not only gave her a referral, but called the person and scheduled the meeting for her.

YOUR CLIENT HAS OWNERSHIP OVER HOW HE OR SHE HELPS YOU

In other words, if it doesn't work, it was your client's idea, and he or she is much more likely to suggest another.

GETTING BETTER RESPONSES

Here's a rundown of some less than helpful responses and ways you can improve upon them:

Should you get the response, "Well, I guess you could call her." No referral system is perfect; there are too many intangibles in human relationships and the way we communicate. If your client suggests you simply call the people you are asking about and you use your client's name when you call the prospects, you only have a 15 percent chance of doing business. So you want your client to warm things up to a 50 percent opportunity so that your calls are expected (see the section "5–15–50–80" in Chapter 1).

Here's what you say: "Would you mind finding out if they'd be interested?" When you say, "Would you mind," people will not object. If they look slightly uncomfortable, it's because they don't know what to say to the prospects—that's what Step 5 is for.

The only other reason they will look uncomfortable is because they do not want to talk to the prospect in question—maybe they had a falling out recently, or maybe they have not been in touch for a long time and it might be too weird to call out of the blue and say, "Hey, what kind of software do you guys use these days?"

In the rather unlikely event they want to know why you want the calls warmed up, explain, "Otherwise it might feel to them like a cold call since they've never heard of me." Everybody hates being cold-called, and so the clients will understand right away.

Should you get the response, "Matt, I have no idea." Sometimes your clients will have no idea. *Then you will need to feed them some suggestions:*

♦ "I'd be happy to talk to your CEO, or to do a brief presentation to your team over lunch, or to join your department for its weekly meeting, and introduce how I might be able to help them."

Or phrase them as questions:

♦ "Do you ever get together for lunch?"

♦ "Would it be easier to meet some of them at one of your weekly team meetings?" (People like the sound of the word *easy* in any of its forms).

♦ "Would it be possible for me to call her or shoot her an e-mail?"

Or you could say:

♦ "Well, what quite a lot of my clients have done is either to set up a workshop in-house or to ask me to stop by so that I could meet their CEO personally."

This approach leverages yet another Robert Cialdini universal principle of social influence, this one being "social proof," which states that *we look to what others do to guide our behavior*. In other words, you suggest that everyone else is having you do a workshop or introducing you to the CEO, and so it would be quite normal for your client to do the same.

EXAMPLE 3

Your client is a manager at a car plant that's doing some downsizing. These are all logical nonsales questions to ask:

♦ "I'm curious: are there other managers at your company in a similar situation to yours?"

♦ "Now I have no idea if you guys ever talk about the financial decisions that need to be made [Step 4], but what would be the best way to find out if they might be interested in discussing some of this?"

♦ "Would you mind finding out to see if they'd be open to hearing from me some time?"

This could lead to being introduced to a boss, other peers, a seminar opportunity, the HR director who doesn't understand the retirement options for employees—sometimes something better than what you might have asked for.

Now you have the name of someone else you can help. Congratulations! You can now move to Step 5 (yes, Step 5, not Step 4).

DO IT!

If names are not popping into your mind right away, your first action is to set a goal to identify one to three prospects in every meeting—people who sound like potential clients and people that your client likes (otherwise your client isn't going to want to contact them).

Practice is the only way you can get to be more successful with Step 3. The proof will be in the pudding because you will be helping your clients think of specific people.

USE STEP 4: REDUCE THEIR RESISTANCE

The purpose of Step 4 is to weave into your Step 3 request the idea that you do not expect your client to know the situation (need or interest level) of your referral request.

Did you notice the number of times that Step 4 was used in the previous two segments? You might want to reread the previous segments again to see how Step 4 is used each time—always the same way.

It brings your request down to earth. It takes any awkwardness out of it. The edge of any neediness is removed; after all, you can't be 100 percent sure the person you're asking about has either a need or an interest; so you can sound more casual.

Here's your challenge: Your client likes you, and of course your client knows people—lots of them. However, each person has a unique situation, and your client certainly doesn't have all the details of the situation—especially as it relates to how you might help the prospective referral.

If you just ask about the needs of somebody in the same life situation or line of work, your client's thoughts may go as follows: "Who'd benefit? My good friend Jeff might ... yeah, but I don't know what he does in this area. We don't really talk about it that much. And what would I say to him?" Your client's doubts start to kick in.

So it usually helps to acknowledge what your client doesn't know; otherwise your client might get uncomfortable bringing it up with someone important in his or her life.

Example 1

"I don't expect you to know what his situation is. Obviously I don't either at this point. What would be the best way to find out if he might be interested?"

Here's how it all moves together:

1. Finish up Step 2, the value conversation.

2. *Then* you get specific, Step 3: *your client's parents.*

3. Now you use Step 4 and reduce your client's resistance: you explain to your client that he may not know about his parents' situation.

4. Maybe you tell a quick story that shows you empathize.

5. *Then you ask!*

And this is what it would sound like:

1. "Mark, I am really pleased this has been so helpful for you."

169

2. "I know you mentioned that your parents live nearby and that you saw them this weekend for your cousin's birthday."

3. "I don't know if you've ever talked to them about what kind of planning they've done."

4. "I know before I got into this business, I never talked to my mother about this kind of stuff. I do remember though how glad I was when I found someone who I could recommend to her just so at least I had the peace of mind she was doing the right thing. I didn't want to stick my nose in her affairs. I was simply saying, I just want to make sure you're taken care of."

5. "Do you know what your parents are doing with their estate planning? (Or, Do you think they might be open to a quick conversation with me about some of that?) What do you think would be the best way to find out?"

You may find this the hardest step to understand and master at first, but there will be times when it makes all the difference. There is something subtle yet effective about it.

Understanding Step 4 helps explain why the once recommended use of the question "Who do you know who ..." usually does not work. Your client does not know whether your referral request has a need or an interest, and so he or she honestly replies, "I can't think of anyone right now," and you get no referrals. Even if the memory jogging produces a name, the name you get is still pretty cold because no need or interest is determined. Remember, it's just a "15 percenter."

EXAMPLE 2

Try humor! Sometimes it pays to make a joke about how nobody talks about your line of work to others by suggesting that normal people talk about it all the time. What's effective about this approach is that it can reduce someone's resistance to bringing it up in conversation.

One insurance agent client once told me that she had said to a customer, "I know you and your brothers are getting together for the Packers game this weekend. I expect when you guys hang out, you probably don't eat pizza, drink beer, or watch the game much, but instead you spend most of the time comparing the deductibles on your homeowners and auto policies, right?"

This got her a slightly dumbfounded look until she started laughing. Then he started laughing too at how ridiculous her comment was. While still in this feel-good moment, she said, "I'm sure they both have insurance [Step 4—no need or interest assumed], but do you think they might be open to hearing from me to see if I could help them if you said something nice about me?"

So that Sunday he told his brothers that he had a new insurance agent who was "really nice and had a great sense of humor," and since that did not describe their insurance provider, they both met with her and became customers too.

RESISTANCE IS FUTILE

There are a couple of other areas where you may need to reduce the resistance of some clients on occasion:

♦ Once in a while, your clients will want to be reassured that everything you've talked about will remain confidential before they refer you.

♦ Very occasionally, people want to know how you follow up with referrals. Maybe they once had a bad experience after referring someone and they just need to hear that you won't be calling their good friend every day.

Only cross these bridges if you seem to come to them a fair bit. Really, all you can do is to be aware of these concerns. As your confidence grows and you know your clients are happy, you are more likely to inquire if you sense push-back from them. That's when you may find out that one of the above concerns needs to be addressed so you can reassure your clients and reduce any resistance.

DO IT!

Start to work in a comment about how you don't expect your client to know about the needs or interest of your referral request. Dare to be funny about it!

USE STEP 5: COACH YOUR CLIENT TO WARM UP THE REFERRAL

The purpose of Step 5 is to make sure your client communicates the right thing to your referral request so that you have permission to get in touch.

You can also do everything right to this point and lose the opportunity because your client says the wrong thing. Don't leave this to chance!

Coaching your referral sources how to warm up their referral will improve your chance of doing business by 35 percent.

I repeat: *Having a name and a willing referral source is often not enough to get a quality referral. You also want to make sure your referral source says the right thing to your potential prospect so that you have permission to get in touch.*

You must have had the experience where a client has agreed to tell someone about you and returned saying, "He wasn't interested." And if you ask your client, "I'm curious ... what did you tell him?" you will likely cringe when your client shares what was said. "I told him you wanted to call him about doing a financial plan for him." "I told him my financial advisor wants to meet him, and he said he already had a guy." "I told him someone I knew wanted to call him about a job selling insurance."

Three Reasons to Coach Your Referral Sources

1. You don't want them to mess it up when you've done everything else right.

2. *Most people have no idea how to refer others about what you do. You must teach them what to say and make it easy for them.*

3. You want them to warm up the referral so your referral request agrees to take your call.

Here's the key to this step: *Keep it simple.* The only job of your referral sources is to open the door and say, "Sophie is great. She's worth talking to. Can she call you?"

They do not need to explain anything about the work you've done. It's not their job, and most people can't explain it well anyway. The more they talk, the more likely it is that the person they are referring will find an excuse or a flaw in their logic and decline.

It's your job to "sell" yourself once the door has been opened.

There are only three ways people can refer you. All these work *some* of the time.

1. In person (this is the best way—especially in a nonthreatening environment, such as over a drink or at an event)

2. In a real-time conversation either over the phone or in person

3. Virtually in an e-mail or through LinkedIn, Twitter, Facebook, etc.

EXAMPLE 1 OF COACHING A REFERRAL SOURCE

This is all you need to direct your referral source's conversation with the referral:

- A strong endorsement of your character or work; e.g., *"You're very pleased with the work we've done."*

- How you want to be introduced; e.g., *"You highly recommend that she at least have a quick conversation with me."*

- Permission for *you* to contact *the referral*; e.g., *"Is it okay if I give her a call some time?"* (Keep this vague.)

This wording is very nonthreatening and does not make you sound needy. Note the third bulleted item: that you are getting permission to call and not letting the referral source simply pass on your business card, leaving you no further course of action but to sit by your phone and stare at it until it rings!

If you specialize in a certain niche market, that's worth including in part a. People would much rather work with a specialist than a jack of all trades:

"Tell them that I work with a lot of people in the gay and lesbian community and that you've been really pleased with the progress you've made."

"Tell them I specialize in helping pharmacists, or people who have just been downsized, etc."

EXAMPLE 2 OF COACHING A REFERRAL SOURCE

Follow up with e-mail or a thank-you note. Having it in black and white can help people remember what to say about you. It also gives you an excuse to "assume" the referral by sending a gentle reminder:

Hi, Gary,

Great meeting you today. Thanks again for talking to your manager to see if she'd be open to hearing from me.

All you need to do is tell her that you've been very pleased with the work we've done, tell her that you highly recommend that she at least have a quick conversation with me, and ask if it is okay if I give her a call sometime.

I'll probably drop you a line in a couple of weeks. Hope your son's basketball tournament goes well this weekend!

Matt

Example 3 of Coaching a Referral Source

You write an e-mail to make it easy for your referral source to open the door. If your introducer is most comfortable e-mailing, it works much better for *you* to write it. People are too busy to take that time, and you can craft your message better than they can.

Here's a more business-specific example used by two of my former clients (two business partners). They ask their referral source (Alan, an accountant) to forward this on to the potential prospect (Sarah):

Hi, Sarah,

I hope life is treating you well since we were last in touch. I wanted to mention a couple of people who are well-connected networkers and who have taken care of several of my clients.

I don't know how pleased you are about all of your current financial relationships, but not only are Brian (Davis) and Simon (Cotton) terrific people; they are also widely regarded as being at the top of their industry.

Their primary specialty is working with owners of businesses like yours. Even if you feel like you have everything sorted, it would still be a good use of your time to meet them.

Would you be open to getting together for golf, lunch, or a drink in the near future with Brian and me? If so, please let me know what dates fit into your schedule.

Kind regards,

Alan

DO IT!

Don't make the mistake of assuming your referral sources have the gift of gab. Get increasingly used to taking charge of teaching them what to say.

Use Step 6: Keep Control of the Process

The purpose of Step 6 is to make sure *you* always have permission to take action so that you can get an appointment with your referral request.

You can also do everything right to this point and lose the opportunity because you turned control over to your client, and by now you are needing to wait to hear from him or her to do something. Don't leave this to chance. Keep control of the process.

You always want to have permission to make the next call to your referral source. Don't just hand out a business card and ask people to pass it on. Don't just *hope* something will happen. Most people's businesses offer important but not urgent products and services.

Example: "When Should I Get Back to You to See If She's Interested?"

Here is why this works.

IT GETS YOUR CLIENTS TO THINK ABOUT
WHEN THEY'LL HAVE THAT CONVERSATION

Also, they will suggest an actual time frame when you should call them back about it—often something like "Why don't you call me in a couple of weeks?" That way, when you do follow up, you can simply say, "You'd suggested this would be a good time to get back to you. Did you get a chance to talk to Jonathan yet?" This is very nonthreatening and makes you simply an obedient professional doing his or her job.

YOUR CLIENTS ARE TAKING RESPONSIBILITY AND OWNERSHIP FOR
THE SOLUTION, JUST AS CLIENTS DO WITH "ASK THE EXPERT"

It is their idea. So if they don't make the call when they say they will, they are much more likely to feel awkward about it because they have not kept their word. They will feel some internal inconsistency.

Of course, this will happen. We're talking about human beings who are not perfect and have other priorities! That's why persistence is so important in asking for what you want. But this process is the highest level of accountability you can get.

IT'S NOT PUSHY

It's not you saying, "I tell you what. I'll call you on Monday at 9 a.m. Shall I call you on your cell phone or your office line? Or would Tuesday at 2 p.m. be better?" Ouch! Avoid sounding needy.

There are two exceptions I can think of:

♦   One exception is if there is a clear reason that timing matters. Perhaps you have an event deadline or a special offer that expires at a certain time. Then you might say, "I'd really like to connect with you before the end of the month, and I'm going to be gone on vacation the week of the twenty-fourth. Is it okay if I get back to you around the nineteenth?"

♦ The second exception is if the clients tell you they will see someone on Friday or over the weekend. In that case, it makes more sense to say, "Okay, well how about I drop you a line early next week then?"

DO IT!

And do not change the wording of the above question. It works really well exactly as it is.

KNOW HOW TO HANDLE OBJECTIONS

Q. How do you handle people who say they can think of someone but want to talk to the person first?

If they are the type of people who want to warm up the referral to make sure it's a good fit, praise them and coach them properly so that they say the right thing. That's Step 5.

If they won't mention the person's name and they are being cagey with you, it's because they are worried about how you will follow up with someone who is pretty important to them. That might be okay too as long as you coach them and keep control.

If they don't really want their name involved, they likely have not been too impressed with you, and you have not really added enough value. I think this is a bad sign.

Or they have had bad personal experiences with someone hounding a referral they once gave, and they need reassurance on this (see Step 4).

Here are some suggestions for those who say they have someone in mind but are less forthcoming:

You: Jennifer, that's great you have someone in mind, and I totally understand your wanting to check with him first. I'm the same way.

(*Try to find out if this person is a qualified referral.*)

You: As you know, the people I can help the most are [for example] companies that lease a lot of cars. What does this person do for a living?

(*She responds.*)

You: Okay, sure. That's great.

You: What many of my clients have found is the *easiest* thing to say is something like, "Greg's a great guy. He's helped my company out a lot, and I really think you should talk to him. *Is it okay if he gives you a call sometime in the near future?*"

(*Now you want to help your client identify a plan in her mind to ask this person before your client gets in her car, listens to her voice messages, turns on the radio, and gets too busy again.*)

You: What have you found is the best way to get a hold of this person?

(*She'll tell you.*)

You: Thanks again for doing that. That's great. When should I drop you a line to find out if he's interested?

Q. How do you handle "I've already talked to him about you," and yet you haven't heard anything?

You: "What did you tell him?"

(*Most of the time your clients' response will explain why nobody rushed to the phone to call you. Return to Step 5 and coach them properly.*)

You: I appreciate your saying something. I think that because what I do is very important but rarely urgent, most people procrastinate on getting in touch with me.

(This lets your clients off the hook without making them look or feel bad.)

You: If you wouldn't mind just mentioning my name one more time; sometimes it's easier to just say, "Kathy specializes in XYZ—she does a very detailed analysis. She really is worth a quick conversation with, and she's super nice. Would you mind her dropping you a line sometime?"

Q. How do you handle, "I gave your name, or card, to …," and nothing has happened?

I am sure you've had e-mails or people that have said, "Oh, I passed on your contact info to a client of mine, or my sister, or some friends of mine at work, etc. Let me know if you hear from her."

It is frustrating because it generally leaves you feeling like there's nothing you can do but hope. Most weeks I am asked by clients, "How should I handle this?"

Here are three suggestions. The real point is to *get possession of the ball* so that *you* can take control of the prospecting process and not have to hope the phone rings or an e-mail appears.

If it's a virtual referral (e-mail, LinkedIn, Facebook, Twitter, etc.), reply with, "I really appreciate your recommending me to your client. *How long do you advise I wait to hear from him?* I find quite a lot of people really procrastinate on getting in touch— and once in a while, they leave it until it's too late!"

Depending on the time that's elapsed, a close alternative might be, "Many thanks for putting in a good word about me to your sister. I've not heard from her yet. *How interested was she?* And how long would you suggest I wait before perhaps trying to reach out to her? I find quite a lot of people really procrastinate on contacting me because what I do is important but rarely urgent."

If it's a real-time conversation, *you could say,* "Thank you for referring me to your coworkers! That's great. *What did you share with them?*" Let the person tell you.

Then ask, "*How would you recommend finding out who is most interested?*" If this person genuinely thinks you do a good job, it really ought to open up more chances for you to take control of following up with legitimate prospects.

The worst-case response would be, "I think they'll call you if they're interested." This gives you a chance to gently inform, "I know, recommending me is a bit like recommending someone to get a physical or to exercise more. It's not like their basement is flooding or their appendix just burst. People know that they should and that it's important, but they find it very easy to put off because it's rarely urgent."

Q. How do you handle, "They said they were already working with someone"?

This one is more complicated because it depends on how happy people are with their current provider and how enthusiastically you were endorsed. If people are on the fence with where they currently do business, a strong endorsement can go a long way to having them consider hearing from you. Sometimes they need to be given repeat requests or to be invited to meet you in a nonthreatening environment.

If you run into this quite often, your best bet is to address it with your clients before they ask.

For example: "I'm sure your friend Margie already has financing with another bank. However, perhaps you could share that the reason people are happy to meet with me is because:

Benefit A

Benefit B

Benefit C

Can you see if she'd be open to hearing from me sometime?"

I recall a recent meeting I had with an estate planning attorney and a financial advisor who were grappling with this. A specific example was being discussed about a client who already had a relationship with a financial advisor.

I pointed out that:

♦ The original advisor did not specialize in working with privately held companies worth between $10 million and $100 million.

♦ Not all people with the same job title are created equal! Were all the teachers you had at school equally effective instructors? Would you ask most third grade teachers to evaluate and edit the content of a Ph.D. dissertation on physics? If the original advisor were that competent, he or she would not have recommended the current (inappropriate) insurance coverage to begin with.

♦ Robert Cialdini's Rule of Authority states that we look to experts to show us the way, and so the attorney's enthusiastic recommendation of the financial advisor he was meeting with would make a big difference!

WHY STEPS 3, 5, AND 6 WORK SO WELL: THE RULE OF COMMITMENT AND CONSISTENCY

The importance of asking your client for advice on the best way to be referred (Steps 3, 5, and 6 of the six steps) is underlined by Robert Cialdini's research and by one of his six universal principles of social influence: the Rule of Commitment and Consistency. This is why it's so important to leverage as much of your client's expertise as possible in identifying the referral, warming up the referral, and advising you on how to follow up.

THE POWER OF YOUR CLIENTS MAKING
A COMMITMENT TO REFER YOU

In a referral conversation, you want your clients to *commit to their idea* (how they think you should contact someone) *rather than submit to yours* ("Can you give me the information and tell the person I'll be calling?").

The more your clients believe that the referral was their idea rather than yours, the more committed they will be in following up on it. This is why the Ask the Expert approach to getting referrals is so effective. ("What would be the best way to find out if Sally might be interested?" or "How would you recommend I find out if other partners at your firm might get similar value?")

Cialdini has found that we are most committed to something that we believe was our decision and that we took responsibility for—and that we did so with no outside pressure (such as being offered a reward or gift, or with your kids it might be a bribe or threat so that they behave).

Other factors that increase your commitment and your client's commitment to following through include:

♦ **Declaring it in public.** Having your client say out loud what she intends to do to contact a referral can go a long way to making sure you get an opportunity to help that person or that group.

♦ **Writing it down.** This is why you've heard so many people endorse writing down your goals. It's been proved to help you achieve them because your commitment increases! And when necessary, you can gently remind a client about information he gave you in writing or put in an e-mail will help nudge him along to follow through. You might bring up his idea by saying, "I'm just following up on something you mentioned in an e-mail you sent to me on the sixteenth. You put in something about how I might want to contact your friend Pauline Jefferson. What would you recommend I do there?"

DIFFICULTY DETERMINES DEDICATION

The harder it is to attain something, the more committed you are to it and the more you value it. This can be anything in life, from pursuing your dream partner and then finding the commitment a no-brainer to training for a marathon and then staying in excellent health. Boot camp in the Marines is so brutal that people emerge "more resilient, simply braver, and better for the wear." Why do you think you see so many Marines bumper stickers on cars? A tough life experience can make people more loyal and persistent.

This is likely another reason why persistence with a prospect pays and why so much business is done because we persist. It was hard to attain, and the bond is therefore stronger.

Finally, this is why some companies and industries find it is worthwhile to bring on new clients by having them make a small purchase. This foot-in-the-door technique works because it leverages the commitment now made. It's why many insurance companies are happy to have you start out buying just car insurance. Once you're a customer, it is easier then to discuss other products and services. It's similar with banks starting you out with checking accounts.

INCONSISTENCY IS AN UNDESIRABLE PERSONALITY TRAIT

One of the key motivators behind our behavior is the need and pressure we feel to be seen as consistent. *So if your client tells you that she will follow up with a referral and she said it sincerely, she will feel awkward about not keeping her word—about looking inconsistent. Knowing this can help you persist in following up.*

SHE GAVE YOU HER WORD!

The power of us wanting to be seen as consistent with our word was tested by psychologist Thomas Moriarty on New York City beaches and written about in Cialdini's book, *Influence*. His task was to find out to what extent people would take their verbal commitment—even if it meant stopping a crime. Here's how his experiment went:

The first time, Person A would find a spot on the beach, lay out a towel, and lounge there for a while listening to his radio. Then he would leave those things behind, and shortly after Person B would grab the radio and hurry off. Only 4 people in 20 challenged the thief.

The second time, a slight twist was added. Person A did the same things, but before leaving he would ask someone nearby to "watch his things." Person B came along and stole the radio, but that was when the unsuspecting watcher turned into a virtual vigilante. This time, 19 of the 20 chased the thief, and some even physically restrained the person or snatched the radio away!

In that instance, there was some danger that people were prepared to face in order to look consistent and honor what they promised. Have you ever been asked to watch someone's stuff? I remember feeling that level of responsibility at a large book shop once when asked to keep an eye on a mother's possessions because she needed to take her young daughter to a different floor to use the restroom.

The scary part is that we will also act against our own best interests to maintain being seen as consistent.

I used to take these step aerobic classes at my gym partly in the hope of meeting eligible women there (okay, almost exclusively in the hope!). Many people who went had their favorite spot to set up their steps, and mine was always in the front row on the right. After some time, I started noticing an attractive dark-haired woman who always would set up in the back row on the left of the gym—a distance I would have no logical reason to stray during pauses in the workout if I wanted to get to know her a little (I later found out she was engaged).

So the next time I went, I set up my steps on the back left row trying to convince myself "It's good not to always do the same thing." But other people noticed immediately and said to me, "Matt! What are doing back there? Why aren't you up front like you usually are?" I actually blushed out of embarrassment because I was being seen as inconsistent. I mumbled something feeble like, "Oh, I just felt like a change." I felt as if I might as well have put up a big sign saying, "Hey, everyone! I'm only back here to hit on this dark-haired woman!" It was almost ridiculous how much it rocked the status quo. So the next time I took the class I returned to the front right row. Being seen as flighty was too painful!

So, remember, commitment by your clients to acting on *their ideas* and to keeping their word can go a long way to helping you get higher-quality and more warmed-up referrals.

The more your clients believe that the referral was their idea rather than yours, the more committed they will be in following up on it.

DO IT!

This week be more open to some of your contacts' advice. Ask them what they think would be the best way to open a door for you. Rely more on their word to come through for you. It may take a little longer, but watch the results. Just don't forget Step 6!

CHAPTER 7

FEARLESS REFERRAL FOLLOW-UP

It's not what you do once in a while; it's what you do day in and day out that makes the difference.

—Jenny Craig, diet guru

KEEP YOUR REFERRAL SOURCES HAPPY AND UPDATED

This is one area in which the vast majority of people do a *horrible* job. Very rarely do people keep their referral sources informed about what happened to their referrals. I understand that it can take a long time between getting the referral and actually meeting that person, but remember that people's integrity is on the line. It is very possible that people who have referred you in the past have stopped because they felt unappreciated since they never heard from you!

I recommend some kind of reminder system or weekly habit to check in and see that your referral sources have been contacted recently. Often they will go to bat for you again!

E-Mail Is Great for Updating Referral Sources

I hardly ever hear about referrals I give to others, and I used to be very weak at keeping others informed about what had happened to their referrals.

I understand that it's difficult—especially when business can take months to develop and phone tag can get frustrating. But we truly do forget that someone once cared enough to refer us, and we owe it to that person to keep in touch. If the person has sent the implicit message that he or she knows, likes, and trusts us enough to refer us, we should be going out of our way to build that relationship. There could easily be more referrals in the future from this person.

Also, a greatly underutilized way to get stubborn referrals to call us back to is to send e-mails like this to your referral source:

Hi, Michelle,
Hope life is good. Just wanted to update you that I have left three messages for your brother over the past six weeks and have not heard back yet.
Any suggestions?
Best of luck with your seminar next week!
Matt

Most of the time in this instance, I find that "Michelle" will feel bad that her referral has not bothered to call me, and she will often respond saying that she will nudge him along; or she may have a good explanation about why I've heard nothing (perhaps their mother has been sick).

This can work well by phone, but I think it is more effective in an e-mail if it's really all I have to say to this person. I often prefer not to interrupt someone's day just to say this. The telephone can be better if you have other things to call about that are adding value to the other person—and if your tone of voice is very patient and casual, like it's no big deal that you haven't heard back yet. If you feel even slightly irritated, stick to e-mail, where, you hope, no one can sense your frustration or disappointment.

MAKE IT A HABIT

The only solution I know of to keep referral sources well informed is to make it a weekly habit as you go through your prospect file.

It's up to you to do the following on a regular basis:

1. Thank your referral sources.
2. Build and mine each of these relationships on purpose.

You only prospect twice: when you feel like it and when you don't.

A SIMPLE SYSTEM FOR KEEPING TRACK OF YOUR REFERRALS

Once you start getting referrals, congratulations! Now you will likely start running into a new challenge—not getting all your calls returned.

Organization now is essential. This is so prospects don't fall through the cracks.

1. You want *one location* with the following information: their contact information, name of referral source, each date of contact (minimum of five—persistence), and the end result. Also be sure to leave room for personal comments, where you can write notes to yourself, such as "Call in a month: just had a baby" or "Ask about their vacation to Mexico."
2. You schedule time to review your prospect list *at least weekly*. This *must* happen (see later on in this chapter).

3. You keep referral sources informed about how things are progressing (see the previous section).

EFFECTIVE FOLLOW-UP CALLS

Sometimes you also need to think of other creative ways to get your name in front of prospects when, say, your voice-mail messages aren't working. Answer the question for that person, "How else can I add value to this person?"

I usually prospect sales managers, and so several years ago I realized I needed to ask myself, "What is important to them? What would help them in their jobs? What should I read more of that has ideas that they would appreciate? What events in their community do I know of that they should know about and might not?"

There are two keys for effective follow-up calls.

KEY ONE: NEVER SOUND NEEDY

In Jim Camp's book, *Start with No*, he reminds us how important it is not to sound needy—that, instead, your calling people is doing them a favor and that you really don't need the business. One suggestion he makes is to tell people:

♦   How much you would like to meet them
♦   That you are not sure if they're interested (if this is true)
♦   That they should let you know either way

This way you sound professional, interested, and not desperate—that it won't impact your livelihood (you are already doing well, and if you're not, act the part in advance!). He argues that this relaxes your prospects, and I have found that when they do feel relaxed, more people get back to me sooner, usually to say that they are still interested. And if they're not, wouldn't you rather know?

A few weeks ago over a stout at a microbrewery, a financial advisor having his best year ever said to me that if he wasn't hearing people say no, he wasn't talking to enough people. That's an empowering mindset.

KEY TWO: USE THE WORD *BECAUSE*

Robert Cialdini's research has found that even when we don't have a very good reason, humans respond remarkably more positively when we give them a reason using the word *because*.

Here is a sample script of a voice-mail message:

Hi, Steve, this is Matt Anderson.
Dave Harper recommended I get in touch with you.

I'm not sure how much he explained to you about what I do; I have been helping him (for example) map out a retirement plan.

(Tip 1) Dave wasn't sure about your situation, and I don't know either. Maybe you no longer have an interest in a brief conversation. If not, just tell me. That's fine.

(Tip 2) But he did recommend us meeting because he's been very pleased with what we've accomplished so far.

I was wondering if we could set up a brief meeting, or have a quick cup of coffee, or grab a quick lunch, and connect on how your financial goals are coming along and see if there's a fit with how I help [or how I work with] business owners like Dave [or young families or retirees or other dentists].

If you could call or e-mail me with two or three times that work for you, either leave me a message at (312) 622–3121 or shoot me an e-mail at Matt@TheReferralAuthority.com.

Thanks, and I'll look forward to talking to you soon.

THREE TIPS FOR MORE SUCCESS FOLLOWING UP

Here are three tips that you should keep in mind as you follow up.

TIP 1. PEOPLE WHO CAN'T SAY NO STRUGGLE TO SAY NO—LOOK AT HOW THEY ARE AS PARENTS

Zig Ziglar has a story about meeting with parents who can't control their kids. He says that if these people cannot say no to their kids, this is a sure sign of prospects that will have a hard time saying no to you. He also says the same for people who do not cancel appointments but don't show up. If they don't have the backbone to even call and say no thanks, they are likely going to have a hard time telling you no when you decide to get in front of them.

TIP 2. FOLLOW UP FIVE TIMES OR MORE—MAINTAIN A PROFESSIONAL TONE

Most people admire those who persist—especially other businesspeople. Your persistence makes a statement that you believe in why you are calling, and the other person's resistance often drops. It does seem that many people's mindset has shifted to one that says "I won't call them back. If they are really keen to talk, they can call me again." The etiquette is simply to leave polite messages each time and call as if it's the first time you've left a message. I really believe it is the tone of our voices that makes a big difference. Sometimes I will mention a date we talked or met so that I come across as professional and organized (and to politely remind the person that it has been a while!).

TIP 3. FIND YOUR HAPPY PLACE TO MAKE YOUR CALLS CONSISTENTLY—USE WHAT WORKS FOR YOU

If you are uncomfortable calling people, find the best time and place for *you* to make your calls. Certainly after a sale is always an easier time to call. For me, it was a long time before I realized I most enjoyed calling people when I was driving somewhere. I felt like I had more of a sense of mission when I was calling while I was traveling, like it was the only time I could call them. There were also times when I enjoyed calling people from a favorite café with a favorite beverage in front of me. This felt more like fun than work.

What to Say When You Follow Up on Your Referrals

Here's the scenario: your happy client, Jennifer, has referred you to Brian, who is a great prospect. If it's a quality referral, then Brian has given permission for you to contact him. In other words, it's a warmed-up referral, which means that 50 percent of the time it should lead to business. Clearly you don't want to drop the ball, but you're busy, right?

What do you do next?

Call Brian

Only e-mail him if Jennifer has told you that that's the best way to contact him. E-mails are too easy to ignore.

If Brian answers the phone:

(*Please note:* In all the sample scripts *every* sentence is there for a very good reason, either to reduce the other person's resistance to meeting or to make sure you don't sound needy in any way.)

Hi, Brian, this is Matt Anderson calling from the Referral Authority. Jennifer Davies put us in touch a few days ago and said that you might be interested in a quick conversation about ways I might be able to help you, or your business. Am I catching you at a good time?

The goal here is to get an appointment on the calendar if Brian is a good prospect for you. So if you need to determine that first, you will ask a few extra questions.

Most of the time, we have to leave Brian a voice message:

Hi, Brian, this is Matt Anderson calling from the Referral Authority. Jennifer Davies forwarded your contact information to me suggesting you might be interested in a quick conversation about ways I might be able to help you, or your business. She wasn't sure if you would be interested, but she did want to connect us because she has been really pleased with the results she has gotten from the work she's done with me. The best time to catch me this week is on Thursday morning before noon, or you can get me next Monday afternoon. Please let me know when would be a good time to reach you in the next two to three weeks.

DELEGATE IF NECESSARY

If you are currently dropping the ball following up, leave the first message yourself and indicate who will be following up instead of you until the appointment is set.

Hi, Brian, this is Matt Anderson calling from the Referral Authority. Jennifer Davies gave me your contact information and said she had talked to you recently about the work that we've done and that you might be interested in getting together some time. Obviously I'm not sure what your situation is and whether there's a fit or not, but perhaps we can find a time to figure that out. You're welcome to try calling me at (312) 622–3121. My assistant, Cloté, manages my schedule, so she would be the best person to call unless you have questions for me. Please give her a call at (847) 850–0510, or I'll ask her to follow up with you in the next couple of weeks.

When your assistant starts the follow-up calls, here are a couple of versions that will ensure that the caller will *never* sound irritated that calls are not being returned and in fact will have the tone of voice that sounds like you are calling for the first time!

Hi, Brian, this is Cloté Smith calling from Matt Anderson's office. Jennifer Davies connected the two of you a couple of weeks ago. I am following up on Matt's behalf because Jennifer had recommended that you both at least have a conversation sometime. I was just calling to see what might work for you in the next two to three weeks. If you could let me know, that would be much appreciated. My number is (847) 850–0510. I hope your day's going well, and I look forward to talking to you soon.

Hi, Brian, this is Cloté Smith calling from Matt Anderson's office. Matt asked me to give you a call because back in April you had expressed some interest to Jennifer Davies that you might be interested in having a brief conversation with him sometime about bringing in more referral business. I don't know if you're still interested or not, and I certainly don't want to keep calling you if you're not (!), but it would be great to hear from you one way or the other. Jennifer has been very pleased with the results she has gotten working with Matt, and we certainly wouldn't be following up if we thought it would likely be a waste of your time. Please let me know about putting something on the calendar or what you would like us to do next—if anything. My number is (847) 850–0510. Thanks, and hopefully we can connect in the near future!

CREATE A TRACKING SYSTEM

The best tracking system will help you make sure that at least five follow-up calls or e-mails are made.

Remember the study of persistence in sales that found that 94 percent of people give up before asking five times for the business, and yet 60 percent of business is closed after we ask five times? Most people call once or twice and give up if they don't hear anything.

If you would like to use the referral tracking system I use, I've included it at the back of this book.

Spread Out Your Follow-Up Calls

I can't say there's a magic wait time between calls. I used to almost always wait two weeks between calls, but sometimes that's a mistake, as we need to strike while the iron is hot. In other instances, people aren't ready to decide or something comes up in their life that is far more important than what we do, and we have to accept that and ask them, "What would you like me to do next?" or "When would you like me to follow back up?"

Alternatively we also need to identify the difference between important and urgent for our prospects sometimes. Many people live a lifestyle now where they see urgency and busyness everywhere, and your job may be to step in and suggest that procrastination may not be wise.

Instill an Empowering Mindset about Following Up with Prospects

The most helpful mindset is to remind yourself that most people admire tenacity because they don't have it! It also helps to remind yourself that some people will hear your messages and say things to themselves along the lines of "Wow! This person really wants my business. He must be pretty confident he can help me. He seems to want to work with me a lot more than the company I currently use."

Honor Your Referral Source

Thank your referral sources and keep them informed. This one point alone is a grossly underutilized strategy to get more referrals. Why do we usually do such a poor job of nurturing our relationships with our referral sources? It's not like there's an unending number of people telling the world about us!

Everyone likes to be appreciated (at least thanked), and sometimes rewarded. Rewards are effective when they are unexpected and personally meaningful to the individual. Last week a client on a group referral coaching call of mine said he had given a referral source a $25 gift card to Menards (a do-it-yourself store). For me that would be about as exciting as getting a magazine on knitting, but when I asked him why he'd chosen that store, he shared that this gift had gone down extremely well because this was the person's favorite place to shop. Perfect!

You need to have a system in place for tracking referrals and referral sources. Remember that you must schedule time to review this list weekly. It's not hard to do and will produce terrific long-term benefits.

Mastering the Big Picture Where Referrals Fit In: Goals and Habits

The big picture of your referral business is the rest of your life and the way it all fits in. There is definitely a time and a place to step back and make sure you are heading in the right direction.

I am compelled to share the time management system I've been using for more than 15 years because so many people blame lack of time as a major impediment in their life. Just last week (at the time I was writing this), a client of mine complained for the umpteenth time that he just never had enough time in his life to do the things he wanted and needed to and—for our purposes—to follow up effectively with the referrals he was working so hard to get in the first place! I offered him some short-term suggestions, but it really starts at the top with being ever clearer about what you want in life.

Today, most people feel that they don't have enough time to do many of the things they want. Dan Baker, in his wonderful book *What Happy People Know*, expresses no sympathy for this so-called belief, pointing out *that there are still 24 hours in every day. He argues that we are programmed by fear to want everything, often because we feel like we are not good enough as we are.*

"The real culprit is making decisions that are driven by fear: choosing too much, choosing a happiness trap* as a priority, or not choosing at all. These are actions that squander time and render it scarce."

His advice is to make sure you prioritize what is truly most valuable to you. The three areas that fulfill us most are our purpose, our health, and our relationships. This leads me back to the big picture.

Goals

This is a great place to start. There are many excellent books on this topic. My favorites are Brian Tracy's book *Goals!*, David Rock's book *Personal Best*, Fiona Harrold's book *Be Your Own Life Coach*, and Stephen Covey's classic book *The 7 Habits of Highly Effective People*. David Rock gets you to have some fun creating short and snappily worded goals that really resonate with you. At present I like starting my day with Brian Tracy's method of writing out 12-month goals in the present tense and starting each sentence with the word *I*. For example, I earn $X, I work out X times a week, I enjoy time with my family X times a year, etc. This is fun so long as you stretch yourself and think bigger with your goals, or else it can get monotonous. The real juice comes from picturing each one actually existing in your life.

---

*The happiness traps are worth listing: trying to buy happiness, trying to find it through pleasure or indulgence, trying to overanalyze the past and end up a victim, trying to overcome weaknesses, trying to force happiness.

I also enjoy John Eliot's contrarian perspective in *Overachievement* that goals can be limiting if you want to be a high achiever. His research with peak performers at Rice University finds that you can get too focused on detail and strategies rather than passionately pursuing the dream, enjoying and excelling at the process, and focusing on what's possible.

The real point here is to create something big that you're up to. Goals based on what matters most to you can get you excited and motivate you in to take action. Remember, it's what they make of you, not what they make for you, that counts. Your business and financial goals can all be impacted significantly by getting consistently more high-quality referrals. That's why you're reading this!

HABITS

Many of us try out new ideas and strategies in our business, and even though we see some positive results, we do not turn them into habits. There are things we did when we first started out that helped us get where we are today—and yet we stopped doing them!

Whether it was because those activities were always outside our comfort zone or because they required greater self-discipline, the fact is we are living small, avoiding complete responsibility, and not fulfilling our potential by avoiding doing these important and effective things.

The book that has influenced me more than any other has to be Stephen Covey's *The 7 Habits of Highly Effective People*. This is information that the growing Gen Y may not be as familiar with. Please spread the word so that the Gen Yers recognize the timeless power of these seven habits:

♦ **Be proactive.** Take complete responsibility for all areas of your life—this is much easier said than done. How's your health? Is there something more you could be doing there? What about your financial situation? Relationships with family members? It's very easy to put the blame "out there" but this resolves nothing.

- **Begin with the end in mind.** Know where you want to go in all areas of your life. When Alice tells the Cheshire Cat in *Alice's Adventures in Wonderland* that she doesn't know where she wants to go, the cat replies, "Well, then, any road will do." Don't be another Alice!

- **Put first things first.** Not pursuing the most important things in life is the cause of most of our unhappiness. You want to spend your time on the first things in your life.

- **Think win-win.** Life and business work so much better when both parties are happy. This is why I believe that asking for and getting referrals should strengthen relationships. Your job is to make sure that the person who referred you is going to get a thank-you and great feedback. Your goal is to make your referral sources feel terrific—not least so they will refer you again, but also to honor the relationships that are being impacted. Everybody's integrity is on the line. How can you grow a business if you're squeezing referrals out of people who are not particularly impressed with the work you've done? It violates every principle out there. That's why you want to ask clients to tell you about the value they have received.

- **Seek first to understand, then to be understood.** Poor communication is the main reason for challenges in life and business. Make sure the other person knows he or she has been understood before you respond. Much easier said than done! For most of us this is a skill to develop.

- **Synergize.** You cannot get to the top on your own no matter how proud you are about being "independent." Reaching out for support and guidance and working together with others will move you from good to great. If you are obsessed with doing it all yourself, you are not at the top of your game. I know, not least because that's how I used to be!

◆ **Sharpen the saw.** This means that if you don't take care of yourself first, you are no good to anyone. You have physical, emotional, spiritual, and mental needs that must all be nurtured and kept active for you to be an effective person.

DO IT!

Start at the top. Make the time to reconnect with what you have identified as your purpose in life and what you value. Every month answer these questions: "What do I really want?" and "What would I do if I knew I couldn't fail?"

Then work on goals that excite you.

This does impact your referral business because it determines your fuel. Without your drive to succeed being connected to your big picture, you won't want to do the work. Start with the Brian Tracy approach to setting 12-month goals in the present tense.

Goals and habits are the first piece to mastering your time and deciding where the referrals you want come into play. There is a second, more strategic piece, and that's weekly planning.

FINDING THE TIME FOR YOUR GOALS, HABITS, AND REFERRAL ASKING: WEEKLY PLANNING

Weekly planning allows you to turn your goals into habitual actions and strategies so that you do put your first things first and stay on top of the referral strategies that grow your business.

Daily planning is too reactive on its own; it focuses too closely on the urgent rather than the important (although I highly recommend Andrew Carnegie's strategy of identifying the top six things each day and starting with the first one until it is complete. He attributed much of his success to this one daily habit). These are strategies I learned mostly from Stephen Covey, Roger Merrill, and Rebecca Merrill's *First Things First* and have personalized over the last 15 years.

First review your goals.

Second, identify your roles in life: spouse, father, daughter, friend, career, volunteer, board member, etc. It is best to have no more than seven roles.

Third, decide what you want to do this week—you do not have to fill every role every week. That will depend on your first things! Put these things on your schedule first. Covey and coauthors call them the "big rocks" that you prioritize by making sure they go on your schedule first, not so that you can pack more into your week, but rather to make sure that they get prioritized.

Then you make room for your next layer of activities. I have developed a list of more than 30 habits that I go through each week. I pause and consider what I am doing in that area and schedule whatever I need to that relates to that area. It helps me enormously in making sure that I put in the big rocks first and that I do not overlook practices that have helped get me to where I am.

My list used to be a few things, and it used to take me 20 minutes. But I have found it so useful—every time I use it, I realize there is something that I cannot afford to forget—that it has become a weekly habit. I recognize it's very detail-oriented, but the benefits far outweigh the time it takes to plan, and I always feel a certain peace of mind when I'm done, that I have a good handle on what's coming up. You will too.

Here is my current list of habits. Some serve primarily as important reminders.

1. Performance and goals review. Set weekly goals out of comfort zone!

2. Schedule workouts, off week (coaching), free day

3. Date night, family time, friends

4. Pay myself first, make tax payments, pay bills, balance books

5. Assignments for my coach

6. Writing time: newsletter, blogs

7. Prospecting time. Track asks!

8. Client prep time and add value to clients' time

9. Presentation prep time

10. Product-making time (CDs, DVDs, manuals)

11. Preplan asks and referral source update

12. Meeting confirmation reminders

13. Networking time

14. Prepare task list for PA

15. Update referral sources on referrals received

16. Personal and professional development (classes, reading time, workshops)

17. Professional volunteer commitments (committees, boards)

18. Association commitments

19. Update managers about groups I'm working with

20. Add value to prospects, key people, clients

21. LinkedIn time, tweeting, weekly pic, quotes and blog

22. Order more books?

23. Hold mail and/or *Financial Times* delivery?

24. Hikes, time in nature

25. Fiction, movie, sports-watching time

26. Birthday list

27. Holiday gifts savings

28. Bookkeeping, mileage to accountant

29. Supplies inventory (paper, ink cartridges, copies, etc.)

30. Groceries and filter change

31. Ironing, dry cleaning

32. Car maintenance

33. Pet care

34. Weekly review

Clearly, you will want to prioritize your own list and add and delete as appropriate. More than anything else, this planning helps to keep you in a proactive mode as often as possible, taking care of things so that there are many fewer breakdowns and last-minute stressors.

The last item, the weekly review, can be very valuable. It takes seconds to skim over each of the past seven days and evaluate what you did at a glance, and it's a great way to be clear on how valuable each meeting you had was. Seven years ago I was in seven different organizations to network. Needless to say, they were not all created equal in terms of helping me grow my business. This quick survey helped me identify where to spend more time. This review is also helpful for one-on-one meetings. There are plenty of nice people out there to have coffee with, but how much do they all impact your business and network?

DO IT!

Make a plan for your upcoming week, including a list of all your habits and everything you want to accomplish. I know this might look like a time-consuming task, but I assure you that planning ahead in these areas makes life much less stressful and, ultimately, frees up time to do more of what you want.

THE TEAM YOU NEED TO GET YOU TO THE TOP

Now that you've got all the information you need to get comfortable asking for referrals and you know when to ask and what to say, will you do it? The odds suggest you may not.

Here's the challenge: *We are a culture of do-it-yourselfers.* Most people think they can do everything on their own—especially once they think they know more or less how. They believe that it is weak to reach out for help and support and that this would make them no longer look good—which is a pretty deep-seated fear of ours!

I used to be one of those people. I worked alone, lived alone, and was 4,000 miles from my family. My favorite personal development book was *Be Your Own Life Coach*; my favorite health book was *Treat Your Own Back* (see a theme here?). Even though my favorite business book was *The 7 Habits of Highly Effective People*, I somehow managed never to apply habit 6—synergize with others and be interdependent. I continued trying to do everything myself. And it kept me small. My only solution was to read more books and work harder. I love reading, but books are not enough.

What you do is all that matters. And none of us are islands. You must have a support team!

Napoleon Hill wrote about one solution in his 1937 classic, *Think and Grow Rich*. He devoted an entire chapter to the importance of the mastermind group and declared that nobody can "have great power" without it! Benefit from the experience, intelligence, and insights of others. You cannot live long enough to figure everything out yourself. And such a group can help sustain your positive emotions.

In Keith Ferrazzi's second book, *Who's Got Your Back*, he writes about developing "lifeline relationships"—which he defines as a small team of individual advisors who give you *feedback, coaching, accountability, and support* to make certain that you flourish.

These four things are what you need to become accomplished at getting high-quality referrals on a consistent basis. This is why top performers (and athletes and performers in the entertainment business) hire coaches.

Why would you want such a team of advisors?

To Go from Good to Great!

First, look at the evidence. In Chapter 1 I wrote about deliberate practice and the fact that almost no one gets to the top without coaching. All the best professional athletes and performers work with coaches. You know this and expect it, although you don't stop to ask why they do and you don't. The problem is you don't think you should get the same, partly because you are not on a multimillion-dollar contract with a pro team or recording company. You make the assumption somehow that it's just for "them"—the superstar superhumans.

But wait! In 2008, Russ Alan Prince's book *The Middle Class Millionaire* revealed that most of the people he studied with a net worth between $2 million and $15 million *did the same thing!* These are not well-known people—just people who have learned from the best. It's time for you to do the same. They are individuals who did not balk at hiring business coaches and consultants to help them in areas that they needed help to go from good to great. These millionaires knew they were not experts at everything, and they realized they did not have the time to be experts at everything. No one does.

They also hired the best legal and accounting help. They hired the top advisors for financial and real estate consulting. Many hired personal trainers—not necessarily because they were out of shape, but because they wanted to reap the four coaching benefits highlighted above.

So it's not just the knowledge. It's finding people who will hold you accountable and point out your blind spots so that you can live a bigger life and fulfill your potential.

1. Your advisors will help you create your own definition of success and will help you develop a plan to get there.

2. The team will help you figure out what you need to *stop* doing to get there.

3. It will provide ongoing support to sustain change (and keep you *out* of your comfort zone).

How do you make these relationships work for you? The four reasons to pursue these relationships are so you end up reaching your goals—whether that's getting more referrals or something else.

SUPPORT

You need people cheering you on—especially those who have no ulterior motive but to see you succeed. Nothing can be more detrimental than key people in your life doubting you at every turn. Reach out to others and ask for more help!

To be effectively supported, Ferrazzi believes that "the secret ingredient to establish genuine lifeline relationships is vulnerability." When you disclose what's really important and talk about your challenges, people can relate to you better—it is likely they have been there too!

A PERSONAL TRAINER FOR YOUR BUSINESS LIFE

Even when we are doing well enough, it never hurts to have someone push us further, knowing that we are capable of much more. It's quite funny: There are many trainers at my gym, and most chitchat with their clients and explain exercises and count reps. Then there is one guy who really pushes his clients and gives them a hard time for not giving 100 percent. He actually gets in their face—although when he steps away, he has a smile on his face knowing it's part of the game. If I were to hire another trainer for myself, it would be a simple choice. He would get me to do my best.

FEEDBACK AND COACHING

One of your problems is you have blind spots that you will likely never see. A good "advisor" will point out these things whether you want to hear them or not. So it is not easy to find such people who will level with you. It's why you want your team to be people who can direct you where you want to go because they either have expertise in that area or can ask you the right questions and inspire you to be motivated enough to take action.

Talking about your fears and obstacles is helpful so that you become self-aware enough to do something differently. Committing to future action and to goals is the public declaration that I wrote about in the last chapter. It makes us more obligated to follow through. That's why I focused so much on knowing what concerns you have about asking for referrals earlier on in this book.

ACCOUNTABILITY

This helps you set higher goals and stretch your ideas of what's achievable. It's one reason why coaching works well. Is your noncoach partner tough enough to follow through consistently with this? Many people are not. Often peers get too close and no longer challenge each other. You will want to frequently remind each other that candid feedback is required.

There are advantages to hiring coaches, because they've worked with many others in the same situation—that's their expertise. It's what they do every day. When it comes to referrals, if I am your coach, I know which direction to go.

There are advantages to having a peer-to-peer advisor: powerful emotional encouragement because your relationship has more depth.

Or have both! Have a coach for one area and a peer for another. Your team can help you put leverage on yourself to "behave" your way to what you want.

WHO MAKES A GOOD TEAM ADVISOR?

Besides a coach with a *proven track record*, think about those people you know who already read business books or invest in attending seminars. This means they already recognize the value of personal and professional development. Perhaps they are regulars in your trade or professional association. In your company it could be your manager or a top performer. Either way, they are people who clearly want more from life and are willing to do something about it.

YOUR BIGGEST CHALLENGE

How you see the world is what determines the actions you take in every area of your life. Any self-respecting personal development book will tell you this. Stephen Covey calls the perspectives *paradigms*. Zaffron and Logan's first law of performance is *"How people perform correlates to how situations occur to them."* Wayne Dyer explains that when you change the way you look at the world, the world you look at changes.

In other words, if you believe that getting referrals will always be tough for you, guess what—it will be! On the other hand, if you believe that getting referrals is something you can do effectively from now on, you will get results from this book.

Warning! Finding the right people for your advisor team is not easy. But as you already know, neither is getting more referrals and reaching your dreams. Pretty much everyone can be bigger in life by finding the courage, guidance, support, and accountability that are often missing. Seek these people out and reap the rewards. I would be happy to be the referral coach for you.

Whatever you decide to do next, take lots of action, persist, keep thinking and asking for bigger and better, revisit what is in this book, and have faith in yourself to know that, with a little bit of help and quite a bit of practice, you can get the results you want and deserve. I commend you for having taken this powerful step. By finishing this book you (really!) have put yourself in a tiny percentage of dedicated professionals. Now it's time to prove that you can fulfill your potential on this one journey on earth.

Weekly Referral Tracker

Asks:					
Referrals Received:					
Obstacles:					
Referral Source:					
Contact Name:					
Phone/E-Mail:					
Follow-Up Dates (5):					
Comments:					
R. Source Updated:					
R. Source Thanked:					
Referral Source:					
Contact Name:					
Phone/E-Mail:					
Follow-Up Dates (5):					
Comments:					
R. Source Updated:					
R. Source Thanked:					
Referral Source:					
Contact Name:					
Phone/E-Mail:					

Follow-Up Dates (5):					
Comments:					
R. Source Updated:					
R. Source Thanked:					
Referral Source:					
Contact Name:					
Phone/E-Mail:					
Follow-Up Dates (5):					
Comments:					
R. Source Updated:					
R. Source Thanked:					
Referral Source:					
Contact Name:					
Phone/E-Mail:					
Follow-Up Dates (5):					
Comments:					
R. Source Updated:					
R. Source Thanked:					
Referral Source:					
Contact Name:					
Phone/E-Mail:					
Follow-Up Dates (5):					
Comments:					
R. Source Updated:					
R. Source Thanked:					

BIBLIOGRAPHY

Abraham, Richard, *Mr. Schmooze*, Hoboken, NJ: Richard Abraham Company, 2010.

Alba, Jason, *I'm on LinkedIn: Now What???* Silicon Valley, CA: Happy About, 2007.

Allen, Robert G., *Multiple Streams of Income*, New York: Wiley, 2000.

Arbinger Institute, *Leadership and Self-Deception*, San Francisco: Berrett-Koehler, 2000.

Armstrong, Lance, and Sally Jenkins, *It's Not about the Bike*, New York: Berkley, 2001.

Assaraf, John, and Murray Smith, *The Answer*, New York: Atria, 2008.

Attwood, Janet Bray, and Chris Attwood, *The Passion Test*, London: Simon & Schuster, 2007.

Bach, David, *The Automatic Millionaire*, New York: Broadway, 2005.

Bachrach, Bill, *Values Based Selling*, San Diego, CA: Aim High Publishing, 1996.

Baker, Dan, *What Happy People Know*, Emmaus, PA: Rodale, 2003.

Bannatyne, Duncan, *Anyone Can Do It*, London: Orion Books, 2006.

Bannatyne, Duncan, Deborah Meaden, Peter Jones, Theo Paphitis, Richard Farleigh, Evan Davies, and James Caan, *Dragon's Den*, London: HarperCollins, 2007.

Beckwith, Harry, *Selling the Invisible*, New York: Time Warner Books, 1997.

Beckwith, Harry, and Christine Clifford-Beckwith, *You, Inc.*, New York: Warner Business Books, 2007.

Borg, James, *Persuasion*, Harlow, U.K.: Pearson, 2010.

Branden, Nathaniel, *How to Raise Your Self-Esteem*, New York: Bantam, 1987.

Branden, Nathaniel, *The Six Pillars of Self-Esteem*, NY: Bantam, 1994.

Branson, Richard, *Business Stripped Bare*, London: Virgin Books, 2008.

Branson, Richard, *Losing My Virginity*, New York: Three Rivers Press, 1999.

Branson, Richard, *Screw It, Let's Do It*, London: Virgin Books, 2006.

Bridge, Rachel, *How I Made It*, London: Kogan-Page, 2005.

Brown, Gordon, *Courage*, New York: Weinstein, 2008.

Brown, Jeff, and Mark Fenske, *The Winner's Brain*, Cambridge, MA: Da Capo Press, 2010.

Brown, Stuart, *Play*, London: Penguin, 2009.

Buckingham, Marcus, *Go Put Your Strengths to Work*, New York: Free Press, 2007.

Buckingham, Marcus, and Donald Clifton, *Now, Discover Your Strengths*, New York: Free Press, 2001.

Burg, Bob, *Endless Referrals*, New York: McGraw-Hill, 1999.

Buscaglia, Leo, *Living, Loving and Learning*, New York: Ballantine Books, 1982.

Buscaglia, Leo, *Love*, New York: Ballantine Books, 1972.

Camp, Jim, *Start with No*, New York: Crown Business, 2002.

Canfield, Jack, *Self Esteem and Peak Performance*, Audio.

Canfield, Jack, *The Success Principles*, New York: HarperCollins, 2005.

Canfield, Jack, and Mark Victor Hansen, *The Aladdin Factor*, Audio.

Carnegie, Dale, *How to Stop Worrying and Start Living*, New York: Simon & Schuster, 1984.

Carnegie, Dale, *How to Win Friends and Influence People*, New York: Simon & Schuster, 1982.

Cates, Bill, *Get More Referrals Now!*, New York: McGraw-Hill, 2004.

Cates, Bill, *Unlimited Referrals*, Silver Spring, MD: Thunder Hill Press, 1996.

Chapman, Gary, *The 5 Love Languages*, Chicago: Northfield, 2010.

Chopra, Deepak, *Seven Spiritual Laws of Success*, San Rafael, CA: Amber-Allen Publishing, 1994.

Cialdini, Robert B., *Influence: The Psychology of Persuasion*, New York: HarperCollins, 2007 (originally published in 1984).

Clason, George S., *The Richest Man in Babylon*, New York: Signet, 1988.

Collins, Jim, *Good to Great*, New York: HarperCollins, 2001.

Colvin, Geoff, *Talent Is Overrated*, New York: Portfolio, 2008.

Covey, Stephen R., *The 7 Habits of Highly Effective People*, New York: Simon & Schuster, 1990.

Covey, Stephen R., *The 8th Habit*, New York: Free Press, 2004.

Covey, Stephen R., Roger A. Merrill, and Rebecca R. Merrill, *First Things First*, New York: Simon & Schuster, 1995.

Coyle, Daniel, *The Talent Code*, New York: Bantam, 2009.

Csikszentmihalyi, Mihaly, *Flow: The Psychology of Optimal Experience*, New York: Harper & Row, 1990.

Darling, Diane, *The Networking Survival Guide*, New York: McGraw-Hill, 2003.

Dudley, George W., and Shannon L. Goodman. *The Psychology of Sales Call Reluctance*, Dallas, TX: Behavioral Sciences Research Press, 1999.

Dweck, Carol, *Mindset*, New York: Ballantine Books, 2008.

Dyer, Wayne W., *The Awakened Life*, audio, Nightingale Conant.

Dyer, Wayne W., *The Power of Intention*, Carlsbad, CA: Hay House, 2004.

Dyer, Wayne W., *Wisdom of the Ages,* New York: HarperCollins, 1998.

Dyer, Wayne W., *You Will See It When You Believe It,* New York: Quill Press, 1989.

Easterbrook, Gregg, *The Progress Paradox*, New York: Random House, 2004.

Eker, T. Harv, *Secrets of the Millionaire Mind*, New York: HarperBusiness, 2005.

Eliot, John, *The Maverick Mindset*, audio, Nightingale Conant.

Eliot, John, *Overachievement*, New York: Portfolio, 2004.

Farber, Barry, *12 Clichés of Selling and Why They Work*, New York: Workman Publishing, 2001.

Ferrazzi, Keith, *Never Eat Alone*, New York: Currency, 2005.

Ferrazzi, Keith, *Who's Got Your Back*, New York: Broadway, 2009.

Ferriss, Timothy, *The 4-Hour Workweek*, New York: Crown, 2007.

Fisher, Donna, *Professional Networking for Dummies*, NY: Wiley, 2001.

Fisher, Donna, and Andy Bilas, *Power Networking*, Marietta, GA: Bard Press, 2000.

Fox, Jeffrey J., *How to Become a Rainmaker*, New York: Hyperion, 2000.

Fox, Michael J., *Always Looking Up*, New York: Hyperion, 2009.

Frankl, Viktor, *Man's Search for Meaning*, New York: Touchstone Books, 1984.

Gage, Randy, *Why You're Dumb, Sick and Broke*, Hoboken, NJ: Wiley, 2006.

Gallup Management Journal, various issues from 2006 to 2007.

Garrison, Steve, *The Five Secrets from Oz*, Charleston, SC: Booksurge Press, 2009.

Gawain, Shakti, *Creative Visualization*, New York: Bantam, 1985.

Gebhard, Nathan, and Mike Marriner, and Joanne Gordon, *Roadtrip Nation*, New York: Ballantine Books, 2003.

Gerber, Michael E., *The E-Myth Revisited*, New York: HarperBusiness, 1995.

Gilbert, Daniel, *Stumbling on Happiness*, New York: Alfred A. Knopf, 2006.

Gitomer, Jeffery, *Little Green Book of Getting Your Way*, Upper Saddle River, NJ: FT Press, 2007.

Gitomer, Jeffery, *Little Platinum Book of Cha-Ching*, Upper Saddle River, NJ: FT Press, 2007.

Gitomer, Jeffery, *Little Red Book of Selling*, Austin, TX: Bard Press, 2005.

Gladwell, Malcolm, *Blink*, Boston: Back Bay Books, 2007.

Gladwell, Malcolm, *Outliers*, New York: Little, Brown, 2008.

Gladwell, Malcolm, *The Tipping Point*, Boston: Back Bay Books, 2002.

Godin, Seth, *Permission Marketing*, New York: Simon & Schuster, 1999.

Goldsmith, Marshall, *What Got You Here, Won't Get You There*, audio, Random House.

Goldstein, Noah J., Steve J. Martin, and Robert B. Cialdini, *Yes! 50 Secrets from the Science of Persuasion,* London: Profile Books, 2007.

Hallowell, Edward, *CrazyBusy,* audio, Random House, 2006.

Harrold, Fiona, *Be Your Own Life Coach,* London: Coronet, 2001.

Harrold, Fiona, *The 7 Rules of Success,* London: Hodder & Stoughton, 2006.

Harrold, Fiona, *The 10-Minute Life Coach,* London: Hodder & Stoughton, 2002.

Hicks, Esther, and Jerry Hicks, *Abraham's Greatest Hits,* audio, Hay House.

Hicks, Esther, and Jerry Hicks, *Ask and It Is Given,* Carlsbad, CA: Hay House, 2004.

Hill, Napoleon, *Napoleon Hill's A Year of Growing Rich,* New York: Penguin, 1993.

Hill, Napoleon, *Think and Grow Rich,* New York: Random House, 1988 (originally published in 1937).

Holden, Robert, *Success Intelligence,* London: Hodder & Stoughton, 2005.

Horsesmouth.com, *Automatic Referrals,* New York: Horsesmouth.com, 2005.

Investor's Business Daily, *Business Leaders & Success,* New York: McGraw-Hill, 2004.

Johnson, Cameron, *You Call the Shots,* New York: Free Press, 2007.

Johnson, Spencer, *The One Minute Sales Person,* New York: Avon, 1986.

Johnson, Spencer, *The Present,* New York: Doubleday, 2003.

Koegel, Timothy J., *The Exceptional Presenter,* Austin, TX: Green Leaf, 2007.

Korsgaden, Troy, *Power Position Your Agency,* Troy Korsgaden, 1998.

Lama, Dalai, and Howard Cutler, *The Art of Happiness,* London: Hodder & Stoughton, 1998.

Lencioni, Patrick, *The Five Dysfunctions of a Team,* San Francisco: Jossey-Bass, 2002.

Lester, David, *How They Started,* Richmond, UK: Crimson, 2008.

Li, Charlene, and Josh Bernoff, *Groundswell,* Boston: Forrester Research, 2008.

Lipton, Bruce, *The Biology of Belief,* Carlsbad, CA: Hay House. 2005.

BIBLIOGRAPHY

Lund, Paddi, *Building the Happiness-Centred Business*, Capalba, Australia: Solutions Press, 1997.

Luntz, Frank, *Words That Work*, New York: Hyperion, 2007.

Mackay, Harvey, *Dig Your Well Before You're Thirsty*, New York: Currency, 1999.

Mackay, Harvey, *How to Build a Network of Power Relationships*, audio, Simon & Schuster.

Mandino, Og, *The Greatest Salesman in the World*, New York: Bantam, 1968.

Maxwell, John, *Thinking for a Change*, New York: Time Warner Books, 2003.

Maxwell, John, *The 21 Irrefutable Laws of Leadership*, Nashville, TN: Nelson, 1998.

Misner, Ivan, and Don Morgan, *Masters of Success*, Irvine: CA: Entrepreneur Press, 2004.

Montoya, Peter, *The Brand Called You*, audio, Nightingale Conant.

Morgenstern, Julie, *Organizing from the Inside Out*, New York: Henry Holt, 1998.

Morgenstern, Julie, *Time Management from the Inside Out*, New York: Henry Holt, 2000.

Mullen, David J., *The Million Dollar Financial Services Practice*, New York: AMA, 2008.

Naisbitt, John, *Megatrends*, New York: Warner Books, 1984.

Penn, Mark J., *Microtrends*, audio, Hachette.

Peters, Tom, *The Circle of Innovation*, New York: Alfred A. Knopf, 1997.

Pine, B. Joseph, and James H. Gilmore, *The Experience Economy*, Boston: HBS Press, 1999.

Port, Michael, *Book Yourself Solid*, Hoboken, NJ: Wiley, 2006.

Prince, Russ Alan, and Lewis Schiff, *The Middle-Class Millionaire*, New York: Currency, 2008.

Rath, Tom, and Donald O. Clifton, *How Full Is Your Bucket?*, New York: Gallup Press, 2004.

Reilly, Simon, *Curing the Unmet Needs Disease*, Saint Peters, MO: Business Building Books, 2008.

Reis, Al, and Jack Trout, *22 Immutable Laws of Marketing*, New York: HarperBusiness, 1993.

Reynolds, Garr, *Presentation Zen*, Berkeley, CA: New Writers, 2008.

Richardson, Cheryl, *Take Time for Your Life*, New York: Broadway, 1999.

Robbins, Anthony, *Awaken the Giant Within*, New York: Simon & Schuster, 1992.

Robbins, Anthony, *Personal Power!*, San Diego: Robbins Research International, 1989.

Robbins, Anthony, *The Power to Shape Your Destiny*, audio, Nightingale Conant.

Robbins, Anthony, *Unlimited Power*, New York: Free Press, 1997.

Rock, David, *Personal Best*, Sydney, Australia: Simon & Schuster, 2001.

Roddick, Anita, *Body and Soul*, London: Vermilion, 1992.

Sanborn, Mark, *The Fred Factor*, New York: Currency, 2004.

Sanders, Tim, *The Likeability Factor*, New York: Crown, 2005.

Sanders, Tim, *Love Is the Killer App*, New York: Three Rivers Press, 2003.

Sandler Sales Institute, *Closing the Sale*, audio, Nightingale Conant.

Sernovitz, Andy, *Word of Mouth Marketing*, New York: Kaplan, 2006.

Shapiro, Stephen M., *Goal Free Living*, Hoboken, NJ: Wiley, 2006.

Sharma, Robin, *Who Will Cry When You Die?*, Carlsbad, CA: Hay House, 2002.

Sheahan, Peter, *Generation Y*, Victoria, Australia: HGB, 2006.

Sher, Barbara, and Anne Gottlieb, *Wishcraft*, New York: Ballantine Books, 1979.

Sher, Barbara, and Barbara Smith, *I Could Do Anything If I Only Knew What It Was*, New York: DTP, 1994.

Smith, Benson, and Tony Rutigliano, *Discover Your Sales Strengths*, New York: Time Warner Books, 2003.

Souza, Brian, *Become Who You Were Born to Be*, New York: Harmony, 2005.

Stanley, Thomas J., *Marketing to the Affluent*, New York: McGraw-Hill, 1997.

Stanley, Thomas J., *The Millionaire Mind*, Kansas City, MO: Andrews McMeel, 2001.

Stanley, Thomas J., *Networking with Millionaires ... and Their Advisors*, audio, Simon & Schuster.

Stanley, Thomas J., and William Danko, *The Millionaire Next Door*, New York: Simon & Schuster, 1999.

Stoltz, Paul G., and Erik Weihenmayer, *The Adversity Advantage*, New York: Fireside, 2006.

Stone, Rosamund, and Benjamin Zander, *The Art of Possibility*, New York: Penguin, 2000.

Switzer, Janet, *Instant Income*, New York: McGraw-Hill, 2007.

Tancer, Bill, *Click*, London: Harper Collins, 2009.

Templar, Richard, *The Rules of Life*, Harlow, U.K.: Pearson, 2006.

Templeton, Tim, *The Referral of a Lifetime*, San Francisco: BK Publishers, 2004.

Thaler, Richard H., and Cass R Sunstein, *Nudge*, New Haven, CT: Yale University Press, 2008.

Thomson, Peter, *The Best-Kept Secrets of the World's Great Achievers*, audio, Nightingale Conant.

Tracy, Brian, *Accelerated Learning Techniques*, audio, Nightingale Conant.

Tracy, Brian, *Advanced Selling Techniques*, audio, Nightingale Conant.

Tracy, Brian, *Change Your Thinking, Change Your Life*, Hoboken, NJ: Wiley, 2003.

Tracy, Brian, *Goals!*, San Francisco: BK Publishers, 2003.

Tracy, Brian, *Many Miles to Go*, Irvine, CA: Entrepreneur Press, 2003.

Tracy, Brian, *Maximum Achievement*, New York: Fireside, 1995.

Tracy, Brian, *The Power of Clarity*, audio, Nightingale Conant.

Tracy, Brian, *The Psychology of Selling*, audio, Nightingale Conant.

Tracy, Brian, *The Science of Self Confidence*, audio, Nightingale Conant.

Welch, Jack, and Suzy Welch, *Winning*, New York: HarperBusiness, 2005.

West, Scott, and Mitch Antony, *Storyselling for Financial Advisors*, Chicago: Dearborn, 2000.

Whitmore, John, *Coaching for Performance*, London: Nicholas Brearly Publishing, 2009.

Wooden, John, and Steve Jamison, *The Essential Wooden*, New York: McGraw-Hill, 2007.

Zaffron, Steve, and Dave Logan, *The 3 Laws of Performance*, San Francisco: Jossey-Bass, 2009.

Ziglar, Zig, *Success and the Self-Image*, audio, Nightingale Conant.

Ziglar, Zig, *The Secrets to Closing the Sale*, audio, Simon & Schuster.

INDEX

About the Author

Matt Anderson, president of the Referral Authority, has grown his business almost exclusively through referrals and now speaks and coaches globally on how to get more and better referrals.

Matt's clients come from a wide variety of financial companies, as well as from sales, law, and accounting firms.

In addition to being published in financial periodicals in the United States, Canada, and the United Kingdom, he has also recorded numerous referral videos and Web casts for professional training organizations.

Matt hails from Coventry, England, and currently lives with his wife, Erica, in Chicago. Visit his Website at www.TheReferralAuthority .com.